From Vietnam to Hawaii

A Spiritual Journey

Linda Liem

ISBN 979-8-89526-723-3 (paperback)
ISBN 979-8-89526-720-2 (digital)

Christian Faith Publishing
832 Park Avenue
Meadville, PA 16335
www.christianfaithpublishing.com

Printed in the United States of America

This is a true story, the story of my life.

Words are not adequate to express my gratitude to the Lord for sending Jesus to save me and sending the Holy Spirit to keep me company while I navigate the treacherous waters of mental illness.

—Linda Liem, RN, BSN, MPH

This book is dedicated to my husband, the love of my life. I remember when we first met.

You were so handsome in spite of your handicap. I could read a good heart on your face. You had a shy smile, and your eyes had that look of tenderness when they rested on me.

Then we were married. We had kids. Throughout those years, we took care of each other in this land, which was not our native land but which carried us and fed us. Our children grew up with the kids in the neighborhood.

Then our people came, the refugees, the boat people of Vietnam. We both were drawn into helping with their resettlement. You got more and more engaged; I pulled back somewhat to take care of our family, the one we created and also the extended one on both sides. The process was unrelented and not like anything we ever imagined.

My beloved husband, when we began life together, we didn't know what the future would hold. The future was not anything I could have imagined.

Then one day I lost you. I was left with our children to hold me together.

Your life was not lost, though. You forgot your own self when you saw the horrors of war and the sufferings of our people. You became their advocate; you threw yourself in the battle of resettlement. It took you further away from your own family as time went by, but it helped those in need of help.

I miss you, but I will see you again in that place of love, where God takes those who have a heart for others.

This book is our story, but it is also the story of our people, a story of grits and tears and a story of hope and redemption and of beauty and glory.

INTRODUCTION

A Prayer

"Oh, Jesus, please give me some toys!"

Everyone was asleep in the room. Mai Lan could talk to Jesus now. Looking at the picture of the doll on the wall, she knelt.

All week, she had cut out, first, the picture of a doll from an old magazine then pictures of other toys, then pasted them on the wall by her bed. The final one, which went above all the rest, was the picture of Jesus. Mai Lan loved Jesus. He looked so handsome and sweet. His eyes gazed directly at her, and his smile promised a cascade of toys to come.

"Jesus, please give me some toys!"

The doll on the wall grew bigger as she fixed it in her gaze, then for lack of anything else to do, she stood up and climbed to the bed.

Mai Lan's family was not wanting by any means. Her father was a teacher, and her mother was a secretary in a government office. They also owned a rubber plantation, which they had started with the money they saved after many years of toiling. They lived in a big three-story duplex in a desirable district of Saigon. She had three meals a day, and snacks in between, and the children were sent to one of the best schools in the country. Nevertheless, they didn't have any toys.

Did she feel deprived? She had lots of fun with her friends at school and after school. They played games with the pebbles picked up from the sidewalks of Saigon. Gathering chopsticks and a tennis ball, they threw the ball in the air and tried to gather as many chopsticks as they could before catching the ball when it came crashing down. They picked the grass when it grew tall enough to cook in pretend pots made of leaves and invented games using tamarind seeds. In short, they were not lacking entertainment. The only problem was that her parents didn't buy any toys. The only reason she could think of was that they didn't think there was a need for toys. Father had grown up in the countryside, the son of farmers, and Mother was orphaned early and shuttled between relatives. Why should their kids have toys?

She looked at pictures of toys and saw many in the windows of big stores. There were oodles of them in the chicest shopping mall in Saigon named Charner at that time. Mother took the kids there from time to time. For Mai Lan, it was like walking into a fairytale.

So she thought, as a last resort, she would ask Jesus for a toy. There seemed to be no other way to get one.

Jesus was indeed looking after her even back then because that Christmas morning, when she woke up, there was a toy under each child's pillow. However, she got a globe made of metal instead of a doll. The globe had all the continents and oceans painted on it. It swiveled around a pivot and could tell her of all the countries on earth when she looked at it long enough. Sister Number Three got a doll. Father and Mother obviously thought Mai Lan was too old to play with dolls. After she thought hard about it, she realized that she hadn't asked Jesus for a doll but for a toy!

For many years, she kept the globe on her desk. She stared at it often, especially when she did homework, and the work got to be too much to swallow. Many years after, when she looked back with nostalgia and tender thoughts to the good times of childhood, she realized that globe had spelled her future. The travel started back then with the globe that Jesus gave her one Christmas.

That was the only Christmas that came with toys. Christmases came and went. The kids grew up.

Mai Lan didn't think of Jesus after that prayer. In spite of unfolding slowly from one day to the next, their lives moved inexorably toward a future unforeseen by all.

CHAPTER 1

Father's Legacy
A Letter

From the house at the end of the village, before dawn, a little boy started walking. With a handful of rice wrapped in banana leaves and slung over his shoulder, he clutched a bag containing his school supplies. He followed a ditch, crossed a rice field, then climbed on a slender bamboo trunk placed over a stream as a bridge, then another rice field before entering another village and emerging on a paved road. Only five hundred meters were left before he reached the school. He arrived at school with the sunrise.

After several years learning Sino-Vietnamese characters from the two teachers in the village, he graduated to the district school. That was a good thing. At noon, he took his rice to the mango tree and broke it into pieces to eat with some salted turnip, which he had also packed in the morning. His eyes were fixed on the dining room where other children sat at tables and enjoyed their lunch of hot rice and soup.

Day in and day out, through the dry and the rainy seasons, he braved the rain and the sun—every day walking five kilometers to school and five kilometers back. At the end of the school year, he passed all subjects with honors, except for French. That was no surprise as his two village teachers knew no French.

He made the trek with his elder brother daily. The difference was that when Elder Brother reached the bamboo bridge over the stream, he stopped to play cards and swim with the kids guarding the buffaloes, then waited for the boy so they could return home. Because of that, Elder Brother remained at home when he reached adulthood and tilled the soil.

As for the boy, patiently, with endurance, he climbed the ladder of education.

One afternoon, Elder Brother accompanied him to school. That afternoon, the boy took a math test that was supposed to last an hour and a half. He came out after forty minutes. Ten minutes after, another student appeared. His brother thought, *Oh no, these two cheated and copied each other's test results. They must be dead!* But no. The boy smiled at Elder Brother to reassure him. What happened was that the boy got the results of the two math problems in half an hour, then reviewed his work carefully and then crossed his arms and waited. The proctors, surprised, went to see what was going on. They looked carefully at his work, talked to each other, then allowed him to exit to the courtyard. He didn't find out until later that they didn't want him to hang around in case some other students got the idea to copy his answers.

That year, he passed the entrance exam for the big school in the city of Tay Ninh. For the first time in his life, he was riding a bus! He had to ride far from his village!

Next he was accepted to the secondary school of Petrus Ky, one of the biggest schools in Saigon.

He remembered placing twenty-second in a pool of close to seven hundred students coming from all over the delta region of South Vietnam. The bright promises of the future now opened widely.

No more long walks to school holding rice wrapped in banana leaves. No more lunches under the mango tree. No watching buffaloes during vacations or planting cucumbers and thinning peanut plants to help the family.

The first history lesson at Petrus Ky guided him for the rest of his life. Looking at a sculpture of four people, he saw a muscled man gazing straight ahead, with a pointed weapon in one hand and a child in the other. The child, although young, showed much resolve. In their shadows were a woman stooping to kindle a fire and a girl holding her shoulder.

The people in that sculpture came into being thousands of years ago in the delta of the Yangtze river. They would follow the boy in his quest for a new life in a new land.

The Viet people went south from the Yangtze river delta and settled five thousand years ago in what is now North Vietnam. There, in a warm climate, were birds singing in the branches, animals roaming the jungle, and fishes swimming aplenty in the streams. Our ancestors left us a beautiful land in the shape of an *S* by the Pacific Ocean. For more than two thousand years, our people had a history. When the boy went to Hanoi for his college education, history was there on the walls of the temples and the monuments dedicated to the many kings and heroes of the past. No inspiration, though, would leave more of an impression on him than the beauty of the girls of Hanoi.

To my children, I want you to know that my destiny had latched onto one thing: mathematics. In 1939, I enrolled at one of the schools in Hanoi training math teachers.

Those days in the North marked my growth into maturity. However, I was born at a time of upheaval and had no choice but to follow destiny.

The French intensified their bombing daily. As a leader in the Vietnamese Scout Association, I worked in the shelters. One day, reaching the shelter and carrying a stretcher with a friend, I found my math teacher lying there, his eyes wide open and his teeth out of their sockets. Some of our classmates were also wounded. Sorrow had caught up with us.

The school was moved to Dalat, a city on the highlands, to escape chaos and destruction. I tried to hang on, moving along with the school. The Japanese army occupied the whole of Southeast

Asia then the French surrendered. The school shut its doors. The war spread to my village. My parents evacuated to Saigon. I quit school, got married, and sold bread for a living to support my parents and wife. Destruction spread across the land, and my family tried to survive.

When the war was over, I went back to school. Since I first began college education, a total of sixteen years had passed. Normally it would have been four years.

But I made it! I had faith in myself.

Up to then, I had many jobs, including selling bread one loaf at a time at the central bus station. After ten years in the teaching profession, my wife and I started a rubber plantation. We do not fear hunger anymore.

When I sometimes drop some grains of rice while eating, I will pick them up in a hurry. I still hear my mother saying, "A grain of rice is a gem coming from the sky. Don't ever waste it!" To all my children, this is the first and the only time I will write you a letter like this. It comes from the deepest part of my heart and is for you, the next generation.

The Vietnamese blood is invincible. Our ancestors fought to preserve our race. We went through one thousand years of domination by the Chinese and one hundred years by the French. We fought hard for our freedom. The sculpture of the man protecting his family and the woman supporting him represents our determination to survive. The present generation must take care of the next one after receiving the spiritual flame handed to them by my generation.

My grandfather earned his living tilling the soil for other people. My father was a medical man schooled in Chinese and Vietnamese healing practices. I am the only one of my generation who made it to college. I expect all of my children to do as I did.

The word is *emerge*.

Father gave this letter to Mai Lan, the eldest of his children, on the evening of her graduation from high school. She kept it throughout her life.

CHAPTER 2

Happy Times

He is coming today.

Mirror, mirror, who is the fairest of them all?

A few steps to the right, a few to the left, turn, turn, swirl.

Look at you, look in the back, look on your side, look at your legs, your dress. Do you think he will like what he sees? My God, this is a nice dress! Isn't it, Mai Lan?

The deep ocean blue of the dress, lightened with turquoise and jade and dotted with shadows of purple blossoms, highlighted her amber skin. The dress was fairly simple. It draped around her slender torso and moved with her as she turned in front of the mirror, falling gracefully from her swan neck and showing off her long legs.

Mai Lan, you don't know what you're dreaming about! Beauty is alabaster skin—so pale that it makes one look like a westerner, so fragile that it reveals one is from a noble family. You are from no noble family. You are just born from the earth, do you hear? Your grandmother toiled in the fields, your grandfather dispensed medicinal herbs to the villagers. When you visited them, you ate rice with peanuts cooked in fish sauce, which smelled like—what else? Just fish sauce, raw fish sauce! So now you think you are a beauty? Excuse me!

Mai Lan's thoughts went back to happy days of childhood when the children piled into the car and headed to the village where she was born. The site of some of the fiercest battles in the war was a picture of peace and quiet back then not far away from Cu Chi, where the Vietcong dug an intricate system of underground tunnels, complete with chambers serving as sleeping quarters, kitchens, and operating rooms. The three-room house in which her father grew up had mud walls and a tin roof and was a haven of relaxation and joy for her and her brothers and sisters. All around the house were rows of mustard cabbage and peanuts. Grandma picked the mustard cabbage plants, washed them in the pond next to the house, and boiled them. Then the plants were dipped in the ground peanuts cooked in fish sauce. Mai Lan forced herself to chew and swallow quickly as she thought of the custard apple trees she would climb as soon as lunch was over. The best times were on those custard apple trees. The forbidden fruit in the garden of Eden could not have been more enticing than those purple and green custard apples dangling from the branches. She climbed one tree, stayed up there until most of the ripened fruits were thrown down to her younger siblings, then got onto the next one and the one after that. When the kids had their fill, she sat squarely on one of the branches with the best custard apple she could find, rolled it hard against her thigh to soften the fruit, then bit into the skin to peel it off and suck on the sweet, milky pulp. Oh, the taste of heaven!

If heaven existed, she wished Auntie Number Three would be there after Auntie passed away. Invariably, the kids ended up at the door to Auntie's room to say a quick hello, then run to the car. Auntie had leprosy. We don't say leprosy anymore; we say Hansen's disease. But back then, it was leprosy. Auntie Number Three sat on her wooden bed, with one leg crossed in front of her and the other pulled up on her side so she could rest her elbow on it. She smiled at them but never said anything. Father said she had to drink a cup of tea sprinkled with gold flakes every day for her leprosy. We kids were not to approach her under any circumstance. In any case, who would want to catch leprosy?

Mai Lan preferred to be like First Uncle. First Uncle had a cubicle-like house by the road on the way to the village. He practiced oriental medicine there. The building had a front room filled with rows of bottles containing all sorts of dried plants and insects, even snakes swimming in alcohol. In the back of the house was a kitchen that Mai Lan never looked in because the front was so fascinating to explore. Father's car stopped there on the way to Grandma's house every time they made the trip. The kids filed out, politely crossed their arms, and bowed low to greet Uncle. He smiled warmly at them, then turned to Father and Mother. While they caught up on the news, Mai Lan went around looking at the bottles, especially the snakes. She shuddered at them but opened her eyes real wide to take in the details while wondering what on earth they could have that would cure people. Mai Lan loved Uncle. One good reason for loving him was that he gave each kid a couple dried prunes to eat at the end of the visit. Another taste of heaven from her childhood.

*****

Mai Lan sighed. She made a few more turns in front of the mirror, checked her appearance carefully, readjusted the bundle of hair piled high on top of her head, then started down the stairs.

I will not give up. I cannot give up. He will be here in about an hour or so. I have long legs. That's right. I measured them a few years back.

There was a picture of Brigitte Bardot in a magazine. She was in a swimsuit. Her legs almost filled the whole picture, so Mai Lan got a ruler, measured them, compared that to the rest of the star's body, and saw to her satisfaction that they were of equal length. She then did the same thing with her own body, and voilà!

I can compare to Brigitte Bardot! My long legs and my smile should do the trick. Maybe some eyelash batting? Do I keep my glasses on, or do I throw them on the table? She sighed again. *This is the first time I see him. I should take a good look at him. Keep your eyeglasses on, you stupid girl!*

"Hello, Chị Năm, did you fill up the teapot? Did you wash the cups?"

"Dear Ms. Mai Lan, he's not here yet. The tea will be cold. Let me take care of it. You calm down. Do you know what's in store for you with this family?"

"He is someone back from studies abroad. He has a PhD, you know! He has brains. He can guide me, he can take me away from this hell. I don't have to watch widows crying for their dead husbands every day on the news, dead bodies in the jungles, dead children in their mothers' arms, dead people everywhere. What a stupid war!"

The maid turned away from Ms. Mai Lan and headed toward the kitchen. "What a commotion! You hear her, and you'd think it's the end of the world!" So it's not the end of the world—not yet, anyway.

It could be the beginning of a brand-new world for Mai Lan if she could shape this encounter to her liking. Her gaze swept the living room. It took almost the whole ground floor of their three-story duplex. The furniture was just standard contemporary, nothing remarkable. She wished there would be some flowers on the dining table, but her mother, for some reason, only bought flowers for big occasions, such as Tết.

Dear me, she only bought flowers for Tết. That's it! At least, the place is clean. I will ask him to be seated on the sofa with his mother. I will be on the armchair across him. What will I say? I don't know what to say.

Mai Lan sat down and relived the talk her parents had with her a few days ago.

"Daughter, listen now. Mrs. Nguyen called. Her son is back here for vacation. He will not stay very long, but he would very much like to see his sister's classmates. Poor son, he had been away so long. He couldn't come back for his sister's funeral. He is still in mourning. Since he cannot see her anymore, he would very much like to have a short visit with her friends. Mrs. Nguyen, of course, wants any relief she can provide for her son. She is a loving mother, in mourning herself. She's already taken him to visit some of your friends, and she is asking to come here as well. We let her know that we would ask for your opinion before giving her an answer."

"Father and Mother, of course, it's yes. I am curious about this marvel of a son who just got his doctorate. He must be an interesting person."

Mai Lan's classmate had passed away last year. They were in college together. Then she dropped out and ended up in France married, dying just one month after the wedding. She took her own life; no one knew for sure why. The family brought her body back home and gave her a big funeral. The whole class was in shock. They went to say goodbye, many of them crying their heart out. She was too young to suffer such a fate. Rumors abounded about her husband's unfaithfulness. Rumors abounded, too, about her mother's manipulation of her betrothal to two men at the same time, and how this created such a tangled web that she ended up paying for it with her own life.

She was a beauty, sought after by many suitors, and a celebrity in her own right at school. She was rather aloof. Mai Lan was not a close friend. When they ran into each other, Mai Lan would have a nice smile, say a few words about the weather or the tons of homework assigned for the day, then go about her day. The elusive beauty usually would be late for class, walk rapidly without looking at anyone, remove the dark glasses she almost always had on, listen to the lectures, and then leave as soon as the class was over. She sometimes could be seen chatting quietly with the male students when she was not late. The women would usually gather to share gossip, shopping tips, and homework in that order but not her. She remained a mystery to Mai Lan.

Mai Lan had no interest in clearing up any mystery. Aside from trying hard to make good grades, she intended to get as much fun as she could out of life. She was twenty years old, out of high school just four years before. Now that she was in medical school, she had her whole life to look forward to. She was smart but reserved and quiet. She didn't have a strong opinion on any subject, and her happy-go-lucky nature netted her a rather large group of friends.

She also wanted to get out of Vietnam. The war had dragged on as long as she could remember and had taken a toll on her family.

Many nights throughout her childhood, her mother was in tears.

"My husband, here's the food. We can eat it all. He is dead. My brother is dead. He is dead, do you hear me? I took this basket to the central jail today. They said not to come anymore."

Mai Lan didn't dare poke her head out to look at Father and Mother, but she could see them very well in her mind—Father with a sad frown on his face and Mother with tears streaming down her cheeks. Mai Lan must have been eight years old then. She tried to hide behind the door because that afternoon, before her mother took the basket of food to the central jail, she stole an egg from the pot of stewed meats and eggs and swallowed it, savoring every bit. That egg was supposed to go to Uncle. He was supposed to be longing for the food because he was in jail, not having enough to eat; and there she was, stealing it from him. And now he was dead! She could throw up that egg except that it was now quite a few hours later, and there was nothing left in her stomach. Poor Uncle! He made it to the south via the Ho Chi Minh trail only to end up in the central jail. They learned many years later that at some point, he was so hungry in the jungle that he boiled a piece of cord to make soup. But, of course, when the war was in full swing, Mother never talked to the children about him. She couldn't trust them to hold their tongues.

After the war was over, they learned he died of a gunshot wound to his back while taking the garbage out at the command of his jailers. He had been captured by the South Vietnamese Army in Cu Chi in a battle between them and the Vietcong. Father and Mother were well established in South Vietnamese society, but Mother's many relatives were fighting for the Vietcong. Mai Lan grew up listening to Auntie Number Six, Mother's youngest sister, talk about how the leader in the North, Ho Chi Minh, would liberate the South and chase all dirty Americans back to America where they belonged. Auntie Number Six would make her appearance from time to time at the home with gifts of oranges or mountain apples, have long talks with Father and Mother, and then disappear.

One time, in a very low voice, she talked about stuffing a doll with some secret documents to pass along to some fighting units. It was obviously not intended for Mai Lan or anyone else to hear, but how do you expect to keep secrets when the house was full of kids running in and out? Mai Lan wished she could understand more of what happened in the grownup world, but she was satisfied with Auntie's gifts and her attention. She loved Auntie Number Six. Auntie told Mai Lan about walking ten kilometers from the outskirts of Saigon to where they lived to save money to buy oranges and mountain apples. With a long ladle made of a coconut shell mounted on a wooden stick, Auntie helped pour water on Mai Lan at bath time. She listened to her stories of playing stick games with the daughter of the Chinese vendor who came every evening to peddle his noodles soup in the neighborhood. Auntie watched as Mai Lan tried out her first fried egg on a small burner in the backyard. They did so many things together when Auntie visited. Mai Lan could not care less whether or not Ho Chi Minh would liberate the South. She didn't hate Americans. She attended a French school in kindergarten and learned in school that her ancestors were the Gallic people. When she was with Father and Mother and her other relatives, she heard that her ancestors were fairies and dragons. Of course, the French descended from the Gallic, and the Vietnamese descended from the fairies and the dragons that gave birth to a hundred eggs. From those eggs, fifty offspring settled in the mountains, and fifty conquered the deltas. To Mai Lan, this history was pretty wild. She knew very well she was Vietnamese, not French. Ah! But the French had so many exciting and fun ways of enjoying life, and they didn't fight and kill each other on the battlefields.

When Americans flooded the streets of Saigon, she found them similar to how she imagined the French. Many of them could be seen in town, parading along Tự Do Street with their girlfriends in tow or passing by in long convoys heading toward the frontlines.

More and more arrived as time went by, and the face of Saigon changed. Sleepy streets woke up with the establishment of bars and entertainment centers; signs written in English sprung up everywhere. Women wore more makeup, their legs revealing more in miniskirts. She heard how easy it was to get a beautiful place to stay when you had an American soldier at your service.

She also kept seeing dead people on the news. Images from the battlefields of explosions, blood, dust, smoke, and body parts appeared every day on the TV screen.

She grew up listening to songs exalting the love between "the young girl left behind and the soldier in the trenches," the sacrifice of romantic love for the love of the country, the importance of waiting for victory, and looking forward to a golden future. In contrast, every day she could also hear songs that were more like sobs and wails straight from the hearts of young widows clinging to their husbands' bodies.

Even before she saw her breasts in her first bra, Mai Lan had made up her mind that she would never be a soldier's wife. A general's wife? Not even. She would be the wife of someone who would not be killed in this stupid war, and that someone could be the person coming to see her today.

*****

Clang, clang! The bell rang at the gate. The maid hurried in and put her mouth close to Mai Lan's ear. "Ms. Mai Lan, it doesn't look good. His mother's lips are clamped on too tight. It's a sign she is a very difficult woman! Do you hear?"

Mai Lan could not care less. *Damn the mother's mouth. What about her son?*

"Did you make the tea?"

The maid didn't answer. She again hurried to the gate and came back with Mrs. Nguyen and her son.

"Hello, Mrs. Nguyen. Hello, sir."

"Hello, Ms. Mai Lan. This is my son, Minh."

"Hello, Ms. Mai Lan. It's very gracious of you to agree to receive us."

Mai Lan forgot to breathe for a moment. He was very handsome. She didn't expect a nerd with a PhD to be handsome. They were mostly a sore lot outfitted with glasses. When they reached middle age, their protruding bellies matched their balding heads. While waiting for middle age, their scrawny bodies seemed to pull ahead of them from all those hours of crouching at their desks. Probably because he was still young, this nerd stood straight. He had a head full of hair neatly cut and a becoming face with large eyes and a gentle smile. The only thing wrong was that he had a slight limp when he walked.

"Mrs. Nguyen and Anh Minh, I am sorry my parents are both at work. They send their greetings and certainly will invite you back another time, but I am so glad to see you. Please have a seat."

It was not until many years later that Minh told her that when he saw her that day, her hair was pulled high, so her neck was like a swan's—slender, graceful, and ready for a kiss.

What a dude! He saw me for the first time, and all he saw was my neck. Dear husband, how was my face? And my body?

That evening, Mai Lan reported to Father and Mother that she hoped he would call again. And he did. After a few more encounters, he flew back to Hawaii. Letters arrived, and she waited for them every day, sitting on the second-floor balcony in the afternoon. She could see the post office worker coming from the far end of the street. Her heart sank when he skipped her house. Most days, though, he stopped and waved Minh's letter at her. Usually, there was one letter. Some days, there were two, even three. They were short notes that repeated the same thing: he thought often of her. Gradually, this changed to him loving her, and finally the proposal came. "Would you consider coming here to Hawaii to marry me?"

"Of course, I would. I've been waiting for this moment for so long."

"Father, Mother, is it okay for me to get married in Hawaii?"

"Daughter, be careful. His sister committed suicide!"

"But I love him. He is handsome, he has a good job. What more can you ask for?"

"What about your studies?"

"I don't care. Girls are supposed to grow up, get married, have children, and be supported by their husbands."

"What about his shriveled leg? Wouldn't you be ashamed being seen with him? What would your friends say?"

"I am not ashamed. If my friends find that one has to be ashamed of a physical defect, then they don't deserve to be my friends. That shriveled leg comes from him catching polio when he was four years old. It's not contagious or anything. It's also why he doesn't have to go to war. I will not end up with a dead husband."

The wedding was set for when Mai Lan could get to Hawaii. Father took off from his busy schedule to visit one of Mother's cousins, a high-ranking officer in the South Vietnamese Army. Mai Lan couldn't explain it, but her maternal family seemed to be full of contradictions. Some fought in the South Vietnamese Army while others belonged to the other side. This uncle of hers in the legitimate government worked his connections. Mai Lan didn't know how much money passed hands in the process, but two months later, she held her passport, complete with a US visa. The visa allowed a stay of three months to get married.

"Kim, look! Look what I have! Look at my passport."

"Oh, for heaven's sake, why are you so excited?"

"I am getting married! I'll go to Hawaii to marry Minh! Wish me happiness! Wish me one thousand years of happiness!"

"Mai Lan, is it real? Why didn't you say anything before?"

"Oh, it happened so fast. He came for a visit, then we saw each other a couple times, then he was gone. But his letters came every day, and here we are. We are getting married—" Mai Lan stopped suddenly when she saw the frozen expression on her friend's face. "What's the matter?"

"I don't know what to say to you. Didn't you hear about the betrothal ceremony between Minh and Hong?"

"What? What's that?"

"Mai Lan, when he came back here, he visited almost all his sister's girlfriends. His parents also arranged for a hurried betrothal ceremony for him and Hong to make official his engagement to her. Why are you talking about you getting married to him?"

Mai Lan grabbed her friend and shook her. "You are kidding me. How do you know?"

Kim knew all right. Her parents knew Hong's family, and Hong's family was friends with Minh's family.

Mai Lan spent many sleepless nights after that.

"What do I do now? You dude, think clearly. How could such a thing be possible?"

Then she recalled. *Damn it! This is more than possible.* She shuddered.

A couple months later, she came home one day to the maid's shocking news. "Ms. Mai Lan, you won't believe this. You will see this beautiful lady at dinnertime. She stepped out of the rickshaw this morning, and she is visiting now with your mother in her room. She looks very distinguished. I have never seen her before."

Chị Năm was right. At dinnertime, the lady was still in her *áo dài*. She was slender. Her face was reminiscent of those paintings of emperors' concubines, and her talk all aimed at finding out how the kids were doing. Father and Mother looked tense and nervous and stayed almost completely silent while eating. The children responded politely that they were doing well in school, listening to their parents as always, and concentrating on making good grades.

The lady left the next day, never to be seen again. After she left, Father and Mother called Mai Lan for a private talk in their big bedroom, which had two sections: one where the bed was and one that was their private sitting room and had several armchairs, a coffee table, some shelves, and a huge wooden wardrobe. They motioned to her to sit down and started explaining. The lady was the wife of Mr. Ly, a high-ranking leader in the Vietcong militia. Father went to school with Mr. Ly, but they were in two separate camps. Father was a good citizen of South Vietnamese society, and Mr. Ly was a leader of the Vietcong. Ordinarily, the family would never have any chance to meet Mr. Ly's wife, let alone have her stay with them for two days. This, however, was no ordinary circumstance.

"Well, guess what? Mr. Ly's wife came to be with us for two days to negotiate something that has very much to do with you, Mai Lan. Her sister knows Minh. Her sister worked as a clerk in the Vietnamese embassy in New Zealand during the time Minh was working toward his degree there. He promised her he would marry her when the time came. So the lady came here to ask us not to proceed with our plan for your wedding. She offered that when the war is over, there will be many high-placed officers in the North Vietnamese Army or the Vietcong guerillas for you to choose from."

"Father and Mother, I certainly will die before I marry any of those men. Can you imagine you sent me to a French school, and I memorized, 'Our ancestors, the Gallic, established France as a country.' Now you expect me to mingle with these people from the jungle? I am not cancelling my wedding by any means. I will go to Hawaii."

Then she forgot the whole episode. It was too stupid, too unexpected, and too bizarre to remember.

So be it. Now what's this nightmare again? Aside from the clerk in New Zealand, now it's this girl from his childhood. Should I just call it quits?

An explanation came with the next letter. Minh's parents were despondent when he came back to visit. They were still in shock over his sister's death. Hong was a daughter of their friends, and both families had always talked about getting the kids married to each other. To help his parents get over his sister's death, he went along with the betrothal, but his heart was not in it. The only girl for him was Mai Lan. He couldn't possibly live without her. "Please pardon my mistake and come here so we can get married. Forget about this incident."

Mai Lan kept quiet about the other girl, the clerk working in New Zealand. Whatever had happened between Minh and that person, it didn't look like he was attaching any importance to it.

If destiny had a face, this was it. The chance to escape from the war and a life filled with fear, the strong pull of the lover with his handsome face and his letters talking of love and an exotic land, plus the promise of much excitement and pleasure—what more could she ask for? She made her decision. Hawaii it would be.

CHAPTER 3

Lunar New Year 1968

The bird away from the branch knows to love the tree and miss its nest
But the communists' invasion only brings calamity.

Mai Lan stopped on the stairs' landing. Her eyes swept the living room.

Mother had been shopping the last few days. The living room smelled like a flower shop. Flowers were everywhere. A spray of red gladiolas on the dining table and several pots of red chrysanthemums and saffron kumquat bushes scattered around the room. On both sides of the altar to the ancestors stood two lacquer jars laden with branches of cherry blossoms. They were the most striking with their delicate five-petaled blossoms of various shades of pink—some fully opened, others still buds.

Each piece of furniture had been polished, the floor scrubbed, even the walls washed. On the altar, pictures of Grandpa and Grandma stood side-by-side looking straight ahead. In front of them, scattered near the edge of the altar, a pair of candles mingled with offerings of five kinds of traditional fruits reserved for Tết, the New Year. Mixed in were incense sticks peeking from bronze holders and ceramic pots of yellow mums next to glistening glass vases full of red gladiolas.

This kind of splendor only happened once a year when the family celebrated Tết. Today was the last day of the old year.

On the stairs' landing, Mai Lan took in the scene. Her siblings had lots of fun times together inventing games to play with household objects. They fought imaginary pirate battles with Mai Lan heading one faction and Sister Number Three in charge of the other. They took turns sliding down the stairs ramp or walking on the balcony's low wall looking down on the driveway. A slip and they would have ended up in the hospital. Their innocence and tender age seemed to defy any instinct to preserve themselves. Thus, they grew up and had lots of laughter, quarrels, and fights. Before Mai Lan knew it, there she was at the threshold to adulthood, ready to fly the nest.

I will remember these happy times of my childhood. This is my last Tết here. Dear me, when will I come back to this house?

Mai Lan couldn't be happier in spite of her inner turmoil.

Minh had returned several days ago. He showed her a pair of diamond earrings and a diamond ring. The gifts came with certificates that had the name of the jeweler, House of Adler, the prices, the center stone's weight, the total weight of the pieces of jewelry, and her name and address. Even the reference number for the diamonds was there.

The price? Thousands of dollars!

Can love be measured by money spent on betrothal gifts? He must love me deeply, my dear future husband.

The third day of the new year, he would come with his parents for the official engagement. No big reception with relatives and friends to share in the happiness. After all, there had been another ceremony with another woman not too long ago.

So what? I will get out of this hell, anyway! No more listening to the news every day and looking at dead bodies. No more widows wailing and kids crying. No more getting lost in novels to float in imaginary worlds where people fall in love, kiss their princes, live in castles, and whirl around in grand ballrooms. Pretty soon, I will be walking the white sands of Hawaii. Minh is so handsome that the girls run after him. Damn it. I love him too.

"Father, do we hang the firecrackers by the front door or outside at the gate?"

Brother Number Four's voice dispelled her reverie, cutting her thoughts short. The smell of food wafted in from the kitchen. Laughter and chatter also drifted in. The family had gathered to prepare for the transition from the old year to the new. The dinner table would be laden with food. Tomorrow would be the same. For three days, there would be nothing but fun, visits, games, a parading in the neighborhood of kids in brand-new clothes, then food and more food—a lot of food.

"Hey, guys, we cannot wait anymore. Let's go upstairs and rehearse. Before you know it, tomorrow will be here."

Mai Lan and the rest of the kids gathered in their collective bedroom upstairs, though the rehearsal was not really needed because every year they carried out the same ritual. Mai Lan jumped to the center of the room and stood straight and tall. One by one, all the kids lined up to her left. When Brother Number Seven, nicknamed Brother Number Last, fell into line, Mai Lan turned her head to see that the line was straight, made sure everyone had their arms crossed in front of them, and said, "Ready?"

All of them bowed their heads low.

"Your daughter wishes you, Father and Mother, another year of excellent health, happiness, and good luck and prosperity."

Going down the line one by one, brothers and sisters repeated the same words with the same intonation.

"Good, you guys, no more rehearsal."

Tomorrow, they would repeat the ritual as soon as everyone was up and gathered in the living room. Father and Mother would reciprocate with a red envelope filled with cash for every son and daughter.

The kids would then sit down for their card games, and everyone would help themselves to the goodies all stacked on the dining table. There would be a lot of chatter about who had earned the most money at the card games, as well as quarrels over who had cheated the most.

About one hour before midnight, Brother Number Four's voice rose again, "Ready for the firecrackers?"

The noise from firecrackers had already started in the neighborhood.

They all gathered by the gates and watched the little red devils light up, dance around, then shatter with a loud boom. Ah! This kind of din must drive away all evil spirits and bring good luck for the new year. The noise continued.

Suddenly Mai Lan's ears perked up. Something was very wrong.

The noise didn't taper off. It intensified, and after a while, it was booming overhead. It turned into a strident supersonic whistle streaking across the sky then a deafening boom that shook the three-story duplex. Father yelled for the children to run back in and stay in the living room. Mother held Brother Number Last in her arms. He was trembling. Mai Lan wrapped her arms around two of her sisters, and the three of them stood bewildered in a corner of the living room. The three remaining kids sat down on the floor.

Father said in a hurry, "Chị Năm, you and Chị Sáu, go upstairs and gather all the mats and pillows. We'll stay here for the rest of the night. Mother, you know where the oil lamps are? I'll get them."

"No, let me get them. Can you find out what's going on? Of all our friends, who would know?"

Father lifted the phone. After dialing a few numbers, he talked for a few minutes, then turned to the family.

"Uncle Tran says his family is spending the night under their beds. The soldiers are everywhere. Gunfire is everywhere too. He had to get out under the bed to answer the phone and said to wait till morning to turn on the radio for information. He doesn't know what's going on."

Uncle Tran lived near the airport where the fighting was probably intense.

The house where Mai Lan, Father, Mother, brothers, sisters, and the maids lived was right in the center of the city. There was no street fighting, which didn't stop the rockets from coming. They all cringed when the strident *eeeek* travelled in waves over their heads, coming from the outskirts of Saigon and getting louder and louder until the rockets reached the central quarters and crashed in a deafening boom on the streets. The earth shook. Then silence came.

All night, they waited. The war had been seen on TV and in the newspapers, but now the war had come to them. It was right here with each and every one of them. Even Brother Number Last knew the war had come. Terror had no loud word but stayed in, walled off by silence.

Terror ate their insides with every screech of the incoming rockets, easing up a bit with intermittent silence then starting again when the next set of noise came. It turned out the oil lamps were not needed much because after a while, the sky lit up as bright as morning, especially where the flares shot high overhead. The light lasted for a while, then gradually subsided as the flares descended and faded away, and darkness took over. Then another corner of the sky lit up. From the direction of the flares, they guessed that events were taking place at the American embassy and the Independence Palace, home of the president of South Vietnam. Gunfire broke out—sometimes intense, other times sporadic. Their home was far enough from the very center of the city that they couldn't hear all that was going on. Enough was heard, though, to indicate that something extraordinary had taken place on the last night of the lunar year of 1968.

They found that out in the morning. The Vietcong in the dead of night, profiting from the setting off of fireworks, had attacked the city of Saigon from all sides and initiated an offensive drive in all major cities of Central and South Vietnam.

Quiet came with the day. While Father and Mother took off to hunt for news and plan what to do with relatives and friends, Mai Lan and the eldest siblings slipped out of the house for a quick reconnaissance of the neighborhood. There was enough noise last night to warrant some exploration. Sure enough, at the intersection two blocks away from home, a huge crater cut deep into the asphalt down to the rocks and dirt underneath. Smoke billowed out from its bowels. Luckily they saw no dead body inside. They stood around on the opposite sidewalk to gaze at the crater for a while, then left in silence. What if the crater had been where their home stood? The rocket could have landed there. It was close enough.

Aside from the crater, everything else seemed to remain almost the same. Pedestrians hurried on the sidewalks with a frown on their face or their lips shut tightly. Cars rolled up to the crater, stopped, and made a hundred-and-eighty-degree turn. Groups of school children passed Mai Lan and her siblings without looking at them. They were obviously out doing the same thing: looking for any trace of last night's events. Ordinarily, a lot of giggling and loud comments would enliven the streets but not today. Faces remained somber. Words could be barely heard, let alone understood.

Father and Mother came back home carrying several large bags bulging with foodstuff. Several dozens of banana hands, twenty cabbage heads, lots of duck eggs—too many to count. Father also hauled in a big bag of rice. All the traditional new year food was still there in the kitchen and should last for the next two days or so, but Mother anticipated that the markets might not open in the near future. She was relieved they could find all the good things they brought home.

"Wow, so many eggs I cannot even count them!" Sister Number Five exclaimed.

Mother explained, "This is better than making meat stew with fish sauce. Those stews don't last more than two days without spoiling. I'll make salty duck eggs. They will last for the next two weeks or so. You never know what's going to happen next. Can you imagine this city being attacked?"

Sister Number Five sat down on the stool next to the table. "Mother, can we stay home from school then?"

Brother Number Four let out a big laugh. "Ha! You want more rockets at night? That's when we can all stay home."

"You may not go to school for a while, but let Father find that out from the school."

For the next two weeks, they survived on bananas, rice, salted duck eggs, and boiled cabbage. The children took turns looking at the eggs bobbing in the big vats of salt water that Mother set up.

The second night of the new year was quiet. The South Vietnamese Army apparently gained enough control that the Vietcong could not fire any more rockets into the capital. The center of Saigon remained calm while the fighting raged all around the countryside.

Mai Lan got a call from the hospital to hurry in. They needed her. Bình Dân Hospital was in chaos when she got there. The waiting room was packed mostly with young men. They were sitting on the chairs and the benches and lying on the floor. Some moaned as they lay on stretchers. The stench of blood mixed with sweat and urine hit her as soon as she walked in.

"Mai Lan, get to the first-aid room."

"Where in hell did all these people come from?"

"Don't you know? The Vietcong took over the roads leading to our city. They are even in the districts on the outskirts of Saigon. Look at the people in the waiting room. You see some bald heads? Rumor has it that they are Vietcong soldiers disguised as Buddhist monks."

Vietcong or not, they needed medical help, and she was there to deliver it. Mai Lan had started her practicum in surgery assistance a week ago. It didn't matter how new or old they were; all the medical students were sorely needed at this time—at least, those who came in. How many of the students stayed home or somewhere else, no one knew.

She changed, masked, and scrubbed, then looked at her first patient. He looked like a teenager. He lay on the table—rigid, pale, quiet, with eyes shut tight. His left leg had a big gash partly filled with dirt. Patches of dried blood caked the edges of the wound.

"Hello, brother. We'll close this cut that you have on your leg. Don't worry, it's gonna heal, and we'll give you something to numb the area so you'll be comfortable."

He didn't answer, but his body relaxed, and he opened his eyes. Squinting under the glaring light at the head of the table, he had the bewildered look of a trapped animal. He nodded slightly, then shut his eyes tight again.

For half an hour, Mai Lan and her classmate injected the lidocaine, cleaned the wound, applied antibiotics, sewed the edges of the wide gap together, applied more antibiotics and a bandage, then got the guy up and out with some oral antibiotics before tending to the next victim of last night's attacks.

Normally they would merely be helping the doctors with such minor surgery, but these were no ordinary circumstances. When Mai Lan finished her shift, the waiting room was still full of people crying, moaning, wailing, and squirming.

She removed her scrubs, changed into street clothes, and climbed on her scooter to head home. In the evening, the family convened as usual.

"Mother, you know what happened today?"

"I hope you're okay."

"Yes, no problem. I helped at the hospital, but guess what, I also helped this country woman by taking her on my scooter to where she wanted to go. She was just standing there at the corner of the street by the hospital. She waved me down and asked for a ride."

"How do you know it was a country woman?"

"She had black pants and a brown peasant-style shirt and a conical hat. Her lips were all red from the betel nut she was chewing."

"Mai Lan, where's your head? What's a country woman doing on the streets of Saigon at this time? Don't you help the enemy in our midst."

Truly, this is a different world. One can trust no longer. Thanks, Mother, for opening my eyes.

*****

That second day of the new year, no friends or relatives came for a visit. Everyone tried to live with the new reality of uncertainty, mostly burying themselves in their homes and hoping for the best. The police set up a barricade of rolled barbed wire. The police headquarters for District Number Three was at the end of the street, just a block away. From then on, only residents of that section of the street were allowed in and out. Mai Lan never saw any fighting. No soldiers were running after each other. No one was shooting. Indeed, there were men in uniforms patrolling with their guns poking out, sometimes pointing at her when she walked by. They looked at her briefly, then went about their patrol. What she experienced of the war was pitiful. Nevertheless, the war was always there.

Curfew came invariably every night at six o'clock. It lifted in the morning for people to go to the market or get to their jobs. Schools were closed, leaving the children to roam the streets for entertainment. There was not much to see, though, after they saw the huge crater two blocks from her street. Mai Lan could hardly wait until evening to climb on the rooftop of her parents' duplex and look toward the airport. From the rooftop, one could see far into the outskirts of Saigon. The first nights after the Vietcong general attack on Saigon, there was a constant stream of refugees from the countryside. It could be her imagination, but their silhouettes appeared to be pressing against each other under the glare of military flares. They looked like marionettes dancing and skipping in long lines that stretched into the night. With the police headquarters right in their backyard, the neighborhood was well protected.

The third day, Minh visited with his parents. They had to park their car beyond the intersection, then make their way on foot past the guard at the barricade bristling with barbed wires. It was fitting that this betrothal formality should be kept hidden from distant relatives and acquaintances by barbed wire.

After Minh and his parents left, Mother sat Mai Lan down and told her how her life started.

"You are a child of war. The night you were born was a night without stars or moon. Father, along with one of our workers, took me on an oxen cart to the midwife's house on the national road to Cambodia. The French were fighting against the Japanese at that time, but the road was completely deserted. We just hoped we would not run into any skirmish along the way. We were lucky we pulled through. We were hoping for a boy, but we love you just the same. Do you know that your umbilical cord was buried there in the yard in front of the midwife's house, and that destiny will have you go back where it was buried sometime in your life?"

Mai Lan started crying. "Mother, I will be in America. How will I come back?"

"Daughter, destiny works in many ways. I am glad you will be away from this land and all the sorrows of war. You are among the lucky ones. Go, girl, and make your life in the new land, and don't worry about us. You will come back someday."

Minh and Mai Lan were able to have dinner together before he returned to Hawaii.

The Continental was about the top restaurant in Saigon. Correspondents from abroad; politicians; businessmen; the military brass, in brief; and the ranking cast of the war gathered there regularly. Mai Lan never thought she would be sitting inside. Now that she had made it there, she sat numbly trying to translate her feelings into words. Minh could not take his gaze off her. She had a simple ivory silk dress, which swayed with her every move. The ivory color set off the subtle glow on her amber skin, which reflected her elation at being with her love. The low cut in the back accentuated her neck, and when he escorted her to their table, he resisted the urge to plant a kiss there. Many gazes followed them as they made their way across the room. The Continental's dining room usually served as a haven for middle-aged men accompanied by young women. Rarely would anyone see handsome young couples. Minh pulled her tighter to his side. She breathed a sigh of relief when the waiter pulled her chair out and bowed slightly, motioning for her to sit down.

Minh took his place across her and asked how she was doing. Recovering from the embarrassment of having to negotiate the dining room under the gaze of a crowd of strangers, Mai Lan launched happily into an account of all she had done these past few days. She kept on chatting throughout the salad, the steaks and *pommes frites*, the banana flambé, and the glasses of wine until it was time to leave, and she realized that Minh had hardly uttered a word.

Minh realized he didn't say much, but he was content just to be in her presence. He had started a job working for a company in Hawaii not long after graduation. His mind was on how to get Mai Lan out of the stupid war as fast as possible.

He had fallen for her the minute he saw her. That minute stayed with him in spite of his mother's relentless exhortations to get settled with the girl the family has chosen. He was sorry he didn't have the guts to resist the engagement ceremony to Hong before leaving the last time and regretted that his engagement had made it to Mai Lan's ears. He was not about to take more risks by stumbling onto some detail that would set his sweetheart off. He was happy looking merely at her and listening to her voice.

That was the norm in his family, anyway. Let the lady of the house talk. Be quiet and listen.

The Continental normally stayed open till the wee hours but not during these times. Guests left early. So did Mai Lan and Minh. When they said goodbye, he reached over, put his arms around her, and planted the first kiss on her neck. She shuddered. A warmth coming from his lips caressed her skin, lingered, and lightened into a thousand tingling points.

"Goodbye, sweetheart. I cannot wait until I hold you again in my arms away from this war."

*****

When the events of Tết 1968 were over, eighty thousand guerillas from the communist side of which a few thousand soldiers from North Vietnam had attacked five of the largest cities of South Vietnam and almost all the local administrative headquarters. In Saigon, nineteen commandos jumped out of two black cars at 2:45 a.m. in front of the American embassy and blew a hole in the side wall. An additional four thousand guerillas attacked various targets inside and around the capital, aiming for administrative buildings, the president's palace, the airport, and residential areas close by.

In Huế, the ancient capital where the last dynasty of the Vietnam kings resided, the attack was particularly bloody. All in all, more than seven thousand North Vietnamese soldiers flooded the city and murdered an estimated two-to-six thousand people whom they deemed loyal to the South Vietnamese government, including health workers and teachers from foreign countries.

The bodies of four German citizens were found near a Buddhist temple. Hands tied in the back with telephone wires, bullet holes piercing their temples from left-to-right execution style, they were buried hastily on their knees in a shallow grave. Doctors Gunther Krainick, Raymund Discher, and Alois Alterkoster were professors at the medical school in Huế. With them was Dr. Krainick's wife, who had been shot the same way. Some mass graves yielded hundreds of people tied together in long human chains. Looking at pictures of mass graves and widows weeping, Mai Lan was more ready than ever to flee her homeland of horror.

On the communist side, the hope to spark an uprising of the masses in the cities against the South Vietnamese government was crushed. Only a fraction of city residents actively supported the government. For the most part, people remained neutral and tried not to take sides.

The events of Tết 1968 marked a crucial turn in the war. For the first time, the people of South Vietnam realized that the enemy was strong enough to be in their midst, whether in rural areas or the cities. They were walking the same sidewalks, getting their groceries in the same markets, living among them, and waiting for the next battle.

Most Vietnamese, however, didn't realize that these events also marked a turn in how the American people viewed the war.

CHAPTER 4

The Vietnam War

I stand on this side of the river
The other side is where the war rages on
My village has witnessed so many years of battle
Each and every bamboo grove bends with grief
O artillery soldier, my friend
Do shoot carefully
Do not touch my home
It's at the end of the next hill
It has vines of bitter melon in front and people I love inside.

From listening to the students in the nursing school at the University of Hawaii, Mai Lan got a taste of what they thought of the war. Could it be that most Americans thought the same way?

The school's classrooms were scattered over two buildings on the mauka side of the Manoa campus. With their backs looking toward the hillsides at the entrance to Manoa valley and their fronts opening to the campus's main walkway, they let the trade winds in all year. Bushes of many colored hibiscus, heliconia, and bird-of-paradise nestled under the hala trees around the school. Lacy ferns caressed anyone passing by with a sweet spicy fragrance that was ever present yet so faint that a person would miss it if too preoccupied with their thoughts.

The most majestic presence was the gigantic monkey pod trees that towered above this luxurious tropical flora. Under them were the smaller poincianas, nevertheless regal looking with their red blossoms bursting in the wind. They reminded Mai Lan of those shading the courtyard in the school she attended when still a child with no worries.

That carefree childhood was gone. She had completed all the forms needed for her registration, paid her tuition fees, and was now heading toward the parking lot. There was no medical school here for her to continue her studies. She would have to apply to mainland schools and, if lucky enough to be accepted, leave Minh to his job and pursue her dream there. *No way. I have him, and I will stick to him.*

Minh too didn't want her to be away. Given her background, the nursing school welcomed her with open arms.

Strolling down the main walkway, she stopped dead at the roundabout by Webster Hall. Circling the roundabout, she saw what seemed like thousands of candles flickering in the gentle breeze flowing from Manoa valley. They were set on the ground. Behind them, hundreds of students stood silently, holding hands and their heads bowed. They were mostly clad in black. Their silence lasted a long time. Finally one of them walked slowly to the middle of the circle and put a megaphone to his mouth to pour out his frustrations with the US policy in Vietnam.

Mai Lan gazed at him intently while thinking of her family back home. Her eyes swelled with tears. Turning around, she kept her eyes fixed to the ground and made her way to her car.

That semester, one of the nursing classes focused on the students' reactions to life challenges. The day before the class, pictures of the Kent State University shooting could be seen in graphic newspaper and TV coverage.

On May 4, 1970, a female student appeared on her knees, screaming in anguish beside the still body of a classmate. Members of the Ohio National Guard had shot and killed four students and wounded nine others. The students had staged a mass protest against the bombing of Cambodia, seen as a widening of the Vietnam War at a time when measures had started to wind it down.

"This is outrageous." Pamela was someone who had not been shy to express her opinion on many subjects. Blond-haired and blue-eyed, she had volunteered in the peace corps before signing up for the nursing school. She was the exact opposite of Mai Lan, who only spoke up when it was impossible to remain silent. Mai Lan knew her English came with a heavy accent and an inadequate vocabulary. To avoid any embarrassment, she kept to herself. She admired brazen people like Pamela just because she had no hope to become one.

Today's class promised to be emotionally challenging. Word was spreading that many colleges would come out in protest against the Kent State University shootings. Of course, Mai Lan, being the only Vietnamese student in the whole school of nursing, would probably be put on the spot and asked to comment on the news. She didn't have any strong opinion on the war one way or the other, reasoning that it was decided upon by all big shots who only cared about their own interests. Since all the nonsense was way over her head, her only desire was to escape the war in any way she could.

She was rather surprised at how the ordinary US citizens reacted to the war. Besides showing much concern over their soldiers being killed for a cause that they deemed foreign to the interests of their country, they seemed to also care for the Vietnamese people's sufferings.

Pamela went on raging against the war.

"Would someone tell me why we are in Vietnam killing old men, women, and children? Have you heard of the My Lai massacre, where nearly five hundred villagers were herded into small groups and gunned down by machine guns? Not one of them was a Vietcong. Where is America's conscience?"

Someone else raised objections. "What about the domino effect? Do you want us to fight the communists on American soil?"

"Still, can we see all these innocent people shot to death?"

"You know, they may seem harmless, but their sons are there in the dead of the night setting up booby traps to greet our soldiers."

"Are we justified, though, to kill these people just to prevent the Commies from invading us? A country without a conscience is a country without a soul. A country without a soul cannot survive."

Then Pamela blurted out, "My dad served in Vietnam. I don't know if I can face him now." A silence fell on the class. Pamela hurried to the door.

Mai Lan fidgeted in her chair. The teacher had earlier gazed at her intently for a few seconds. The silence lengthened.

What about my father, mother, sisters, brothers, and my whole extended family? We are all trapped in this situation at the mercy of Americans fighting for their interest. She feared the students' movement. She feared what would come next.

Pamela came back and settled in her chair. She kept her eyes downcast. They were red. Mai Lan shuffled in her chair.

These poor young people of America are all mixed up about their feelings. Mistakes happen in wars. Horrible ones. Does that justify pitting children against their parents? Vietnamese children honor their parents and support them in what they do. American children obviously have other values they take into account.

Her own outburst surprised her.

"Pamela, you know, your dad is your dad. He brought you to this life, raised you, fed and clothed you, and gave you an education. Please think of what he did for you. Whatever else he did in this life, remember that and love him."

After class, Pamela invited Mai Lan for a get-together with her and her friends. Mai Lan politely declined.

"Sorry, Pamela, I won't fit in. Don't you see, I am from this far, far away place."

CHAPTER 5

Marital Bliss

Who brought the mynah bird across the river?
She escaped her cage, put her wings together, and flew far away.

Not too long ago, that faraway place said goodbye to Mai Lan.

Everywhere was blue. Under the clear blue sky was the deep blue of the vast ocean, and scattered in it were the jewels of the Hawaiian Islands, dotted with the green of mountains and forests. The sun illuminated the landscape beneath the wing of the Continental Airline plane. Mai Lan was in heaven. She thought of pinching herself just to make sure she was not dreaming.

It felt like ages ago, but it was just yesterday that Mother helped pack her wedding *áo dài*, which consisted of two dresses—the one underneath made of white silk and the one outside, all-white lace. She couldn't find a veil in Saigon. Luckily, the wedding wouldn't take place until a week after the day she arrived, so she would have time to find one.

The whole family saw her and Sister Number Four off at the airport. The friends who had left before her to study abroad wrote about many feelings of sadness at leaving the country of their childhood, but Mai Lan didn't feel anything like that. She was simply elated at her escape. Father saw fit to send Sister Number Four to serve as her bridesmaid. Sister Number Four could profit from the occasion by pursuing her studies in America since she had already been there as an exchange student. This added to Mai Lan's elation.

I miss him. I want to feel his embrace, his pecks on my neck, his hands on my skin. What's the matter with this plane? It's taking forever to depart.

The wait was even longer in Guam, where they refueled. Now the plane was rolling toward the terminal.

When she finally emerged from the cabin, she stopped for a few seconds at the top of the stairs, drawing a deep breath in. The sweet, gentle Hawaiian air caressed her skin in a warm embrace. The air smelled faintly of the sea, not like in Saigon, where a mix of various scents, good and bad, always seemed to hang heavily.

Where is he? Her gaze swept the walls of the terminal. She would have to clear the customs first.

"Oh, my dear sweetheart!" He was right there by the gate with a big smile on his face. "Sugar honey, you look wonderful! Good trip?"

"I feel dizzy. It's been a long trip. Glad I made it. How are you?"

As she fell into his arms, the dizziness vanished. The melody of "La Vie en Rose" hummed softly in her ears.

*****

At lunch, she got her first taste of an American hamburger.

"At long last!" she exclaimed to Minh. "You know how long I waited for this hamburger? When Sister Number Four came back from California after her year in the student exchange program, I asked her to make a hamburger. I had seen them on TV, the cooks flipping them on an open fire and people looking at them with eyes that seemed to pop out of their sockets. Sister never made one. She told me there was no hamburger bun that could be found in the whole land of Vietnam, outside of American establishments. So I've dreamt of hamburgers for several years now."

"Sweetie, the American way is to add lots of ketchup, also pickles and mustard."

She followed all instructions, took a bite, grimaced, and put it down. The pickles were too sour. The ketchup and mustard added a foreign taste unlike anything she had ever eaten.

Minh took a bite of his hamburger contentedly and kept on looking at her, but he seemed oblivious to her fidgeting in her chair.

The next day, he took her to his workplace cafeteria.

"I don't want you to cook. We can come here and eat, so this should save you a lot of work in the kitchen."

"You spoil me! I can cook, you know. I learned how to cook when I was just starting high school. I thought no one would want to marry someone who cannot cook."

She indeed spent much time in her parents' kitchen following the cook and asking many questions about why things were done the way they were. Then she tried her hand at washing the veggies first and cutting them and graduated to cleaning fish and helping with the meals.

She did get to cook all she wanted after one week of cafeteria fare. The ham was served with pineapple, the poi tasted like glue, and the rice was mixed with strawberry jam to make dessert. In Vietnam, pineapple was used in soup. Poi was unheard of, and rice was eaten with savory dishes. At the end of the week, her mouth felt dry, her lips were chapped, and she couldn't bear to look at another cafeteria dish. Through it all, she hung on at Minh's side and concentrated on learning all the English words, which poured out in a gibberish nightmare of sounds.

*****

The wedding took place at Honpa Hongwanji Buddhist Temple on Pali Highway. Mai Lan saw it once before the ceremony. In Vietnam, Buddhist temples have ornate roofs, entrances adorned with red and gold columns and courtyards filled with urns in which incense burns. In Hawaii, the temple looks more like a mosque. The whole building is white. The courtyard has neat markings for cars to be parked. There are no urns, incense, smoke, or ornate columns. Mai Lan breathed a sigh of relief when she entered the sanctuary and saw a statue of Buddha at the far end of the room. In front of the statue stood an altar filled with flowers and candles. And yes, there were incense sticks too, filling the air with a familiar sweet scent that, for her, was the essence of a Buddhist temple. She looked around and wondered what her family would say when they saw pictures of the sanctuary filled with neat rows of chairs. She could hear them: "Sister Number Two, were you married in a church or a temple? How come there are so many chairs in there? The temple is supposed to only have mats on the floor. You're sure you were in the right place?"

Other than the veil, which she had the luck of buying on the day after she arrived, she had no control over the wedding. Minh had mobilized his colleagues and his friends and thought of pretty much everything.

It took place on a hot afternoon in August. She walked down the aisle on the arm of Minh's boss. They were surrounded by his colleagues and friends. They signed the wedding certificate in a room in the back of the sanctuary, witnessed by two friends of the groom and Sister Number Four. Even with Sister at her side, Mai Lan missed her family. Aside from Minh and Sister, the people at the wedding were strangers.

Minh's boss was gracious enough to lend his home for the reception. Beyond the front gate was a small yard adorned with an antique well as picturesque as those seen in old English landscapes. White and pink plumeria flowers floated on its water. Red and white balloons swayed gently in the breeze blowing from the valley. In the living room, a banner displayed Minh and Mai Lan's names intertwined in an oriental calligraphic pattern. So from now on, they were one.

On the tables were spring rolls, papaya salad, roast pork, finger sandwiches, an assortment of pastries, and a huge plate of cut fruits. Mai Lan looked with fascination at the pink punchbowl spewing out a steady stream of smoke. Her student life in Vietnam did not expose her to such sumptuous celebrations of life. She barely touched the punch after discovering the taste of rum lacing the juice.

I've got to stay in control and figure out what people are saying.

A few Vietnamese people mingled with the other guests. She tended to take refuge with them but made an effort to greet everyone and learn a bit about their roles in her husband's life, trying to decipher what she could of the English that floated all around her. Minh also concentrated on his exchanges with his friends and colleagues, seeming to forget she was at his side.

Her eyes sometimes lit up while carrying on conversations with her husband's acquaintances. At other times, they swept the room to take in all the beauty of an exceptional American home. She felt like she had graduated to something very big. Her first night in Hawaii was also the first night she hadn't heard any gun or rocket noise. Today was the first day of her life with the person she had most longed for these past two years. And yet deep inside her, an emptiness remained unexplained.

That vague, uneasy feeling changed into panic toward the end of the reception. After the guests departed, Mai Lan looked at the wall. The banner bearing their names was no longer tacked on it. One side had become detached and hung down, hiding Minh's name. Was the banner not attached properly? Or was it a portent of things to come? Some bad omen? She shuddered and clung even more tightly to Minh's arm.

Sister Number Four was pretty familiar with life in America and had no problem mingling with Minh's friends. In fact, instead of hanging around the two love birds, she disappeared most days with Minh's friends. After her departure to a college on Maui, Mai Lan started missing her family badly. Mai Lan couldn't help but wonder why Minh didn't keep her around instead of sending her away. Resentment crept in, but she resolved not to dwell on it.

They made their love nest in the one-bedroom apartment that was part of the soldiers' barracks lent to the company Minh worked for. The one-bedroom unit was just right for the newlyweds. Minh realized that there was no need for a honeymoon trip since Mai Lan was still experiencing culture shock, so their first month together was a continuous trip around the island of Oahu, stopping here and there to marvel at the beauty of the sea and the mountains.

She concentrated on enjoying her new life with a doting husband in a land of milk and honey, away from gunfire, dead soldiers, and wailing widows.

In his company, she tasted a grasshopper cocktail for the first time before getting into his embrace for a slow dance. Around the island, he planted a kiss on her lips at every beach as if to mark those stops for eternity. At gatherings with friends, remarks abounded on how he had changed for the better. Of course, he no longer lived on cans of pork and beans. He had a cook and went back to savoring all those wonderful dishes of his childhood. He had Mai Lan swimming with him at Queen's Surf almost every afternoon after work. Mai Lan could pinch herself raw. She was living a dream.

*****

Ala Moana beach promenade had a crowd of people today. The balmy weather was just the right kind of warmth brushing the skin like a lover's hand. The sun got ready to settle for the night, slowly descending on the horizon in the west. A big ship made its way from the harbor, its silhouette cutting into the sun's orange glow. Several newlywed couples struck poses against the sunset. A lone man with a ukulele hummed "Tiny Bubbles," then blared out his baritone voice over the waves. Sitting on the low wall that ran the length of the beach, Minh and Mai Lan drew close to each other.

The waves rocked them into an embrace that felt like heaven.

"My darling, in your arms, no harm can come, right?"

"Cherie, I love you. Life is not life without you."

Two kids ran by, chasing each other and shrieking in delight. Mai Lan turned sideways, following them with her eyes. Minh followed her gaze.

"Darling, can you see our kids chasing each other down this promenade?"

"I haven't thought of kids yet. You are all I want."

"But, Minh, it would be so sad without kids. I have lots of siblings. It's fun."

"We'll think about kids later, sweetheart. I feel like going for a swim. Shall we jump in?"

"You go right ahead. The water's too cold for me now. The sun will set soon."

Minh jumped up and started toward the restrooms. Mai Lan watched his back getting smaller as he crossed the street and made his way through the park adjacent to the beach. He was so tender and loving. She had never heard him complain about her cooking. The only way she could tell he didn't like what she served was when she saw him get up and fetch some butter from the refrigerator to mix in his rice. Rarely would she see anger in his face. When things weren't quite right, rather than tell her what was bothering him, he would hold it in. The next day, he would be his normal self again. She didn't think much about asking what bothered him because she was the same way, preferring to weep at night by herself when thinking about the family that she left behind.

When Minh came back, a young man was standing in front of Mai Lan. The young man left as soon as Minh approached. Minh looked sharply at him.

"Mai Lan, what was he doing standing in front of you?"

"Oh, he just asked me for the time."

Returning home, Minh drove onto the sidewalk with the wheels screeching against the pavement. Mai Lan sat frozen in fear.

Why in the world does he behave in such a way? He can get us killed driving like a madman. Could he be jealous? She could have asked him for an explanation. Instead, fear discouraged any discussion, and the incident slipped to the back of her mind.

They continued touring the island, savoring the taste of salt and sea in the wind. She experimented with marrying her native dishes with the local ones to Minh's delight. She felt secure and safe in their love nest.

Minh had many friends in the Vietnamese community, so the couple was invited to many birthday and wedding celebrations.

Happiness continued even when she found out she couldn't enroll in medical school because Hawaii didn't have a full-fledged medical program. She would have to fly to the mainland USA. A nursing program would be an acceptable replacement.

So instead of being a doctor, I will be a nurse. So what? The kids will come. Dear husband, how many kids do you want?

*****

Mike arrived three years after Mai Lan set foot on this land of the brave and the free. He said hello to the world at Kaiser Hospital on the south shore of the island of Oahu. Mai Lan could not take her eyes off this jewel that the heavens sent her. He had a perfectly shaped face, all ten fingers and toes, and her heart just melted looking at his mouth when he sucked in his lips.

From her hospital bed, Mai Lan could look out over the Ala Wai Yacht Harbor.

Am I on an island in paradise taking a vacation? My dear Mai Lan, you must be the luckiest of them all. Can you believe this hospital setting?

Her grandmother, following tradition, slept on a cot with a hibachi underneath to keep her warm after giving birth to her children. Back then, they believed old age would come with lots of aches and pains for women who dared not let the fire warm them after giving birth.

Having had to spend sleepless nights in the tropical heat until she figured out sleep would come with her body on the cool tiled floor, Mai Lan shuddered at that barbaric practice. Luckily her mother balked at tradition and saw fit to follow her inclination to lead a more liberated life.

Now that Mai Lan joined the succession of women in the family, she got up for a shower the day after Mike was born. She spent most of her time playing with the drawer that served as a crib for the baby. On the other side of her room was the nursery, which was the hub around which the new mothers' rooms revolved. Many cribs could be seen through the glass windows. They were actually drawers that could be pulled out into the new moms' rooms or pushed back into the nursery at the mothers' convenience.

Mai Lan was delighted with the arrangement.

Even more joy came with Minh's visits. His grin didn't seem to ever disappear when he entered the room and greeted his son. Minh never dreamt he would one day have a son, mostly because of his handicap. Although the limp had nothing to do with fertility, the thought of being inferior because of his defect was so deeply ingrained in his psyche that it colored his thinking and influenced his actions in almost every aspect of his life.

Minh took a week off from work, looking at and babbling to Mike after they brought him home. It took him a few days before he got the courage to hold his son in his arms and carry him around the room. From then on, between taking over some of the household chores for Mai Lan and driving the new family around on excursions near and far, he doted on his wife and son.

Mai Lan couldn't have asked for more.

CHAPTER 6

The Hell of 1975

Thousands of flowering stems bending in the wind, birds tired of flying
Hundreds of willows glistening with dew, traveler quickening his pace
One staying home, one far away
Where is the one to share stories with?

"Congratulations!"

Mai Lan looked at her. Her beautiful daughter swaddled in a light blanket looked back. Her rosy cheeks were graced with a dimple by the mouth. She had ten perfect tiny fingers. Mai Lan would uncover her later to take a peek at her toes, but for now she could not take her eyes off her baby's face.

Four years ago, Mike had come into their lives. Their first bundle of joy had drawn many comments from friends as to how he looked so much like Minh. He brought joy and blessings with every step in his development. Now a preschooler, he brimmed with energy and laughter. It was time for a new addition to the family.

Minh had decided to go back to Christchurch for his sabbatical. They were now at the very place where Minh began college.

The day after Malia was born, the nursing students at the Wooden Valley Hospital filed one by one into Mai Lan's room to look at the baby's abundant black hair. They told Mai Lan they had never seen a baby with so much hair and black at that. Caucasian babies have practically no hair when they are born, and this hospital was in a place where Mai Lan guessed people had seen Asian babies rarely, if at all.

Mai Lan was well-tended to. The food was excellent, varied, and plentiful. She would get hungry regularly before mealtimes and listen with anticipation to the food cart approaching her room. One of the blessings of nursing one's baby was being able to eat one's fill without gaining weight. Her milk overflowed for the baby. This time around, she knew what to expect and was more relaxed.

It was a blessing that Malia weighed in at seven pounds, eleven ounces, full term. About two months ago, Mai Lan had been in this same hospital for a few days to stop a premature labor. The room was dimly lit to facilitate rest and relaxation. Mai Lan was under orders to keep to her bed. Luckily, the contractions stopped after the first day, and she was elated to come back to her son who had been left in his dad's care. Looking back, she felt it had been stupid to iron the sheets after laundering them, the cause of the premature contractions. But then, she felt so good, full of life and energy, in that dreamy autumn weather in Christchurch.

Her body obviously didn't agree with how she felt. A month after being hospitalized, her blood pressure shot up, and her feet started swelling, which prompted the obstetrician to diagnose preeclampsia and induce labor. Labor was pretty fast with the IV continuously stimulating contractions. The waves of pain came very close to each other, leaving her no time to rest in between. The baby emerged quickly. *So here she was, my little angel.* No bliss could compare to what Mai Lan felt when the baby was in her arms.

Until the third day in the hospital, Minh gave Mai Lan the morning newspaper after she finished her breakfast. The headlines blared trouble. The Communists were in Central Vietnam, their army marching South and pushing inexorably on. Highway 1, the main artery of Central and South Vietnam, used to transport all supplies alongside the South China Sea, filled with people fleeing the terror. Day by day, cities fell to the Communists. Day by day, Mai Lan went over the newspaper in horror.

On March 11, her baby came into this world. The same day, Ban Mê Thuột in the Central Highlands was taken by Hanoi general

Văn tiến Dũng. Huế, the capital of Central Vietnam, fell on March 25.

One week after Malia was born, Dad and Mom took her home. Mai Lan hugged her son tight, having missed seeing him greatly. He had missed her a lot, too, and didn't appreciate the presence of a stranger who took so much attention away from him. He hadn't understood why, all of a sudden, Mom had disappeared again. He was cranky and clung to her. The family was reunited now, except that what should have been absolute happiness had shadows of sorrow lurking in the background.

Now it was not only the newspaper. Practically every TV screen blared scenes from the Vietnam War. Mai Lan ended up cradling Malia in her arms and watching the news on TV most of her days. Brother Mike, feeling left out, climbed into the bassinet sitting on the floor, took refuge there, and refused to budge. Mai Lan had no energy left to cuddle him and tell him he counted too. At night, she dreamt he was abandoned in a ditch to fend for himself. Try as she might, she couldn't get to the ditch to rescue him. The dream recurred for what seemed like days, and yet she couldn't figure out what to do.

Aside from feeding her husband and kids, Mai Lan seemed to have lost her energy. The apartment went to seed. Toys, pots and pans, and sheets and clothes were scattered throughout the home. Her zest for living was replaced by feelings of hopelessness, anxiety, and anger.

What will happen to my folks once the Commies take over? My father, mother, sister, and her husband and kids? The rest of us are abroad, but they are not safe.

The Northern army took Đà Nẵng then marched on to Saigon. Highway 1 was littered with bodies of civilians who fell in exhaustion or who had been shot. Smoke, fire, debris, long trains of people carrying baskets dangling from bamboo poles, kids clinging to their mothers, men bent under elderly relatives they had on their backs, loaded cars and massive tanks—all mingled on the highway.

The coconut wireless talked about Vietnamese overseas hopping on planes to go back in the hope of getting their relatives out before Saigon fell. Mai Lan pondered how she could do such a thing too, then looked at her two kids and thought of what would happen to them while she was away, of the chances of her being stuck there, maybe forever. Who would take care of them? She could wean Malia in a hurry. Her husband could care for them, though it had always been her handling this part of their lives. What about the neighbors? They barely knew them. Bob and Jane, Minh's good friends, maybe? Could Minh go back instead of her?

Minh tried another way. Every day he was at the American embassy in Christchurch. He sent several wires to the embassy in Saigon every day, stating that they were American citizens and asking the embassy to get their relatives out. The wires listed the names of Mai Lan's parents, her sister An, An's husband, and two kids. Luckily, Minh's side of the family, his parents and sister, already had visas for the US. They had planned on a visit to Hawaii and obtained them before this hell happened. They would have no trouble getting out.

Luckily, Minh's cousin worked in the American embassy as a clerk. She was in the section responsible for issuing visas. Many years later, she told them the room where she worked was filled to the ceiling with cables from all over the world. It was a miracle she could dig out one of the cables that Minh sent and complete the paperwork to get Mai Lan's side of the family out. In the meantime, Mai Lan's anxiety and feelings of despair continued.

Mike was in preschool. Every morning, she took him there, walking across the lawn between the buildings that housed members of Minh's company. Every lunchtime, she walked to the school to retrieve him. Malia stayed in her crib during these daily trips, and Mai Lan worried about the baby when she was not under her watchful eyes.

All was not gloomy despite feelings of being so lonely, so lost in this part of the world. Christchurch's fall season was beautiful. Most trees turned manifold shades of yellow and rust. Even the sunrays were gentler, the air sweeter. The edges of life seemed smoother as if nature had seen human suffering and decided to help.

When Mai Lan walked around the buildings with her son, they would spot mushrooms sprouting in the grass. "They are just the white mushrooms you see in the supermarkets," Minh said the first time they came across the sprouting stems. He urged Mai Lan to pick them and cook them, but she had read too much about people dying from eating wild mushrooms to listen to him.

There were rides to the countryside to admire the fall setting in. Bob and Jane, friends who resided close by, visited from time to time for a chat.

The month of March ended, April came, and the situation in Vietnam worsened by the day—scenes of chaos, people fleeing, dead bodies on the roads, smoke, and fire everywhere. There were deafening bomb crashes, cries of terror, and wails of pain. Mai Lan couldn't bear to see so much suffering on people's faces. The despair in their eyes haunted her nightmares. Then it was April 30.

The whole world watched the first Communist tanks crash through the fences surrounding the Independence Palace where South Vietnamese president Nguyễn văn Thiệu, having fled, resided. He was replaced by an interim president, Nguyễn văn Hương, a figure head who was waiting in the palace to surrender to Hồ Chí Minh.

Minh and Mai Lan were on edge. No news of either side of the family emerged. They watched with horror as helicopter after helicopter landed on the American embassy rooftop to pick up the last Americans and those Vietnamese people who somehow climbed through barbed wire to ascend to the spot.

The helicopters worked around the clock and deep into the night, ferrying people onto warships waiting in the China Sea. The noise of the helicopter rotor blades was deafening.

Then the last one took off into the night. The final shot on the TV screen showed desperate Vietnamese looking up at the sky in an eerie silence.

About a week later, they got news that Minh's parents and his sister had made it to Guam. They were among the first ones out, thanks to the visas they obtained beforehand. Minh told them to continue to Hawaii and wait for him and his family. Then he put in his request to his company for a premature return to Hawaii.

Mai Lan notified Mike's schoolteacher that they were leaving. She reminded Mai Lan that when she registered him for school, she was told it had to be for the whole semester. With the little English under her command, Mai Lan tried to explain the situation, only to receive a dirty look. What a shame! The dirty look followed her for a long time.

The plane back to Hawaii had two hooks on the partition wall right in front of their seats to hang the bassinet for Malia. The baby slept the whole trip.

Minh was elated at the thought of being reunited with his parents and sister, but not Mai Lan. Her mother-in-law had made her promise to come back to Vietnam after they got married. Of course, they could stay in Hawaii for a while, but the family had just lost a dear member and would be so happy to have them return. They never did go back, and it seemed to Mai Lan there had to be some kind of reckoning because of the broken promise.

*****

Mai Lan's thoughts drifted back to those times when life was dolce vita. Those times, the only worries were how to get the best grades in school so she could still boast of being the best student, or the best nerd, depending on how you looked at it. Back then, nothing compared to vacation time, especially when it meant walking around under the pine trees in places that looked like European mountain resorts.

Mai Lan ran into Mrs. Nguyen and her two daughters while rounding the corner of a pathway in the pine forest.

"Hello, my friend, what a nice surprise!"

"Hello, Mai Lan, nice running into you too!"

Her friend's mother smiled at her. A bit on the heavy side in her long black pants and loose silk tunic, she had a welcoming look on her face. Mai Lan didn't particularly think of old people as beautiful, but this mother of her friend had large brown eyes that shone and a warm smile. Her whole person seemed to be eager to get to know her.

She waved Mai Lan to sit down by her side, displacing her two daughters from the bench, and proceeded to inquire about Mai Lan's parents' health and her experiences at school.

What a nice lady! Mai Lan thought.

That was Mai Lan's recollection of her first encounter with Mother-in-Law.

The second time they met was after her daughter's suicide. She visited with her son in tow, fresh from New Zealand. She was a changed woman. Strain and stress had taken a toll. Her lips clamped tight when she didn't speak. Her eyes did not shine but looked dull and tired.

"Mai Lan, my son has no chance to see his sister now, so it's a consolation for him to see his sister's friends."

Mai Lan did not pay any more attention to Mother-in-Law's looks. While waiting for the relationship between her and Minh to solidify, what she perceived of the grief that had taken over this family made her uncomfortable. She, therefore, concentrated on carrying out the old lady's requests, be it running errands for her or helping with light household chores. When she was ready to travel to Hawaii, Minh's family saw her off at the airport along with her own family.

Now they were on the plane flying back to Hawaii and heading to God knows what. Much water had flowed under the bridge of time. Minh's family had lost all their wealth and a whole country. So had Mai Lan's family.

*****

"My granddaughter!"

Mai Lan handed the baby to Mother, who took a long look at her. Mike was almost a clone of his dad, but Malia rather looked like Mai Lan. Was it disappointment that Mai Lan read in Mother's eyes? A thought implanted itself in Mai Lan's mind. *I hope she does not think Malia comes from the mailman.* Mai Lan suppressed the thought in a hurry and joined the family's celebration.

Chatter, smiles, laughter—it was happy times in spite of their world being turned upside down. Minh's parents and sister were delighted to see the grandkids, nephew, and niece and relieved to have escaped the war and the brutal yoke of the Communists.

As for Mai Lan, she put on a happy face for everyone's sake. Days ahead would be stormy. That inner anxious feeling had not left her ever since they boarded the plane.

The families settled in a spacious four-bedroom rental. Rather, it felt more like Minh's family settled themselves in the spacious house, with Mai Lan taking on the role of maid.

Ever since setting foot in Hawaii, Minh's family had been subsisting on rice and eggs because those were the cheapest foods they could find. Before leaving the old country, Mother sewed a few hundred dollars in the hem of her shirt. The rest of their fortune was now sitting back in South Vietnam, gone. Their diet improved significantly when Mai Lan took over the cooking.

She tried her best to be a good daughter-in-law by catering to every member of the family, as Vietnamese tradition dictated. She had no idea what was in store for her as time passed.

The day they moved in, Mother looked at the bedrooms and assigned them. Of course, the master bedroom went to Minh and Mai Lan because they were still the main providers, but Father and Sister didn't have any say. Then Mother took a rag and began cleaning the bedroom that was to go to her daughter. Kim, in her early twenties, hung around, doing nothing. She even had to be reminded to use the bathroom before leaving the house. Not that she didn't know, but Mother had to express her love in some way. As for Father, he just waited for things to be finished.

Minh got back into his job. On top of that, being that there were so few Vietnamese people settled on the island, he was called by the state to help with the refugees who kept on passing through Hawaii before flying to the mainland to resettle. As a result, he was never home. He only showed up when he had to pick up his folks to do the paperwork needed to resettle them.

All household chores fell on Mai Lan. She had a preschooler and a baby to take care of. A big house to keep clean. Five adults to feed. She also helped out with her in-laws' resettlement paperwork. They were used to having maids cater to them in Vietnam. On top of that, Mother seemed to think Kim was still a baby. It was true that they had experienced a whirlwind of disturbing emotions. Anxiety, fear, sadness, loss of all their possessions, indeed loss of a whole way of life, compounded by distrust of Mai Lan, made for uneasy cohabitation.

Recalling the promise she made to Mother to bring Minh back home after their marriage, Mai Lan tried to make amends.

She bought a nice present for Kim. Kim opened it while on the way home from the shopping center, and it flew out the car window. When Mai Lan complained that she couldn't handle all the housework by herself, Mother had Kim mop the floor once and take the baby out in a stroller once. Then Mai Lan was told that was quite enough.

One night, Mai Lan woke up with a feeling of dread. Sitting on the bed with her heart pounding, she tried to make sense of the way she felt. Nothing out of the ordinary had happened the day before. Hoping the feeling would go away with some diversion, she got out of bed and opened the bedroom door. Lights were on in the living room. Mother was there, sitting on the corner of the sofa, a pile of pictures in front of her. She was holding Mai Lan's picture and had torn it in half. The tear passed through Mai Lan's smile; half her face hung limp. The picture dangled from Mother's quivering hand. Mai Lan jumped across the living room and yanked her picture away.

"How dare you!"

Cradling the picture in her palm, she retrieved the others from the coffee table and retreated to her bedroom in tears. *How could she do such a thing!* That was Mai Lan's favorite picture. She was sixteen back then. Done at a studio, the photograph captured her amber-colored skin and her radiant smile. Her face had been photographed at an angle, and her eyes had that special light of innocent tender age when one looks to the future for a life full of promise.

Mai Lan sat on the bed with tears streaming down her cheeks.

On the other side of the bed, Minh slept without a stir. The explanation for this weird behavior, if Mai Lan could pull one out of the deep recesses of Mother-in-Law's mind, resided in something she was told not too long after.

"When I first lived with your father and his family, I made it a point to go to the back of the house if my mother-in-law was in the front and vice versa. Do you know that your father is always chasing after the girls year after year?"

Could intense feelings of being neglected shape a desire to be the only one who mattered in her son's life? And to cling to her two kids for survival? Even to the point of keeping her daughter tied to her and not allowing her to grow up?

Then something else happened. Mother had this habit of saying her Buddhist mantra while sitting cross-legged on a mat in a corner of the living room every morning. She would sit with her eyes shut and slowly run through her beads while murmuring a short mantra in Sanskrit. The whole thing usually lasted about fifteen minutes. That particular morning, a huge cockroach appeared out of nowhere and ran around the mat like crazy. Mother was blissfully unaware of the cockroach, but Mai Lan couldn't stand seeing it. She ran to the kitchen, came back with a broom, and chased the roach around the mat. Mother opened her eyes and said, "Don't you kill that roach. Buddha teaches 'Thou shall not kill.' Let me say a prayer so the roach can be reincarnated into a better life form."

Mai Lan decided to look for a place for her in-laws to move to. She lost so much weight those past few months that now she walked around like a skeleton. She had no time and no energy to eat. No joy was left to subsist on.

After Minh's family moved out, he didn't talk to her for two months. They turned into zombies—him burying himself in his work and her in her house chores and childcare.

Being the only son in the family, he was expected to take care of his family. Since family rules precluded loud arguments and anger was a forbidden feeling, it was best not to acknowledge the rift. He simply decided to shut Mai Lan off from all he did for his family. In the meantime, Mai Lan's family landed in Hawaii. The load of worries doubled, but for Mai Lan, relief came with the love brought by her parents. There was also a whole community of Vietnamese people in Hawaii to help out. Minh's services were very much in demand. The majority of Vietnamese on the islands knew him. He was their ambassador, their spokesperson, the one who negotiated settlements for them.

Those times were a blur of upheaval, tears, and pain—quarrels between family members, hurt feelings on all sides, and a lot of physical and emotional turmoil. And yet it was also a time of excitement with so many changes happening, a time of thankfulness for staying together. They lost no one to the Communists.

A time of much hope for the future.

CHAPTER 7

The Split

Who split the moon in half?
Half printed on the lone pillow case
Half shining on the miles of roadway.

The future came but was not what they could foresee in their wildest imagination.

"You come with me and close this account."

Mai Lan's mind went blank. How in the world did he find out?

"I just wanted to set aside a bit of my earnings to help my family. You know, not anything big, but my folks are still struggling. Most of my siblings are still in school. You know that most of my salary goes into our account, don't you?"

"Your folks have been here for a while already. We cannot continue to support them, don't you know that?"

So the account was closed.

Since the beginning of their life together, Minh had always been the one balancing the checkbook and controlling their finances. Mai Lan felt smothered by this marital life. Day in and day out, she couldn't breathe, feeling as if an elephant was sitting permanently on her chest. She tried to take deep breaths when she felt particularly choked, especially at night, only to have the weight descend on her again.

Life became a routine of work and domestic chores. Her nursing job did not provide for much flexibility, so Minh picked up the kids after school and took them to their grandparents. They doted on them. Mother even thanked Mai Lan for bearing grandchildren for her. Mai Lan missed the irony of it until she finally realized many years later that she was considered a childbearing machine whose role was to continue the lineage.

Minh's work with his company and the community did not leave him any time to spare. Behind the scene, mother wielded her magic wand to gather her son to herself, so more and more, he spent time at her place with the two kids.

As to Mai Lan, she hung on to her friends for comfort.

"Mai Lan, we are glad your sister-in-law is getting married."

"What are you saying?"

"Don't you know? It's all over Chinatown that she is getting married to this guy fresh from Vietnam."

Mai Lan stopped eating. Mai Lan and her friends were around a table at Pho 77 in Chinatown. Her friends all knew things were not going very well between Mai Lan and her in-laws, but this looked to be beyond repair.

"What are you going to do?"

"What can I do? My life is hell now. What do you think I should do?"

No one around the table ventured any suggestion.

"I certainly will not attend the wedding. I am not informed, nor am I invited. I am through with this family. Mother-in-law has her son, but I don't have a husband." So since Minh buried himself in his work and spent his spare time with his family, she might as well find solace in hers.

*****

Palolo Valley Homes is the home for a sprawling community of immigrants on the island of Oahu. The Vietnamese were the latest group to join a bustling assortment of Samoan families. Laotians and Hmong also joined the community.

Palolo Valley is one of many such valleys on the island of Oahu that begin deep on the flank of the Koolau mountains and run to the ocean. While other valleys may be settled by the wealthier class of Honolulu, Palolo is not. Here, one is greeted with a Hawaii of yesteryear, when people still lived close to the earth.

The buildings, which stand in the middle of the valley, were almost uniform in their air of neglect. Instead of looking at them, Mai Lan concentrated on the space between them. Various trees and shrubs seemed to sing of the joy of creation. From what grew in front of the dwelling units, one could tell for sure where the people inside came from. Ti plants mixed with heliconia and bird of paradise nestled under banana and breadfruit trees—the residents were most certainly Hawaiians or Samoans. Shrubs of Thai basil and crawling mint along with red pepper and sugar cane—the residents were Vietnamese or Laotians or Hmong.

Mai Lan took care of the elderly men and women suffering from an assortment of ailments, as well as young families brimming with toddlers and babies. She loved the people here in this valley.

One of the nurses in her office had the habit of writing an inspiring thought on the office board every morning when the staff started their day. Many of these were taken from the Bible. Mai Lan often drew strength from them.

This morning, the words on the board did not make much sense.

"'I fed you with milk, not solid food, for you were not ready for it'" (1 Corinthians 3:2).

"Talofa, Mrs. Manayan!"

"Oh, it's you. Come on in."

Mrs. Manayan's living room was a bare space with a mat covering the entire floor. To Mai Lan's amazement, the mat made of woven lauhala looked exactly like the ones she sat on when she visited relatives back in her native land. It was the only furniture in the room, if you could call a mat furniture. There was nothing else. Mai Lan had visions of bedbugs crawling underneath the mat. Nevertheless, she sat down on the floor. There may not be any bedbug at all. Anyway, she was here to work on lice, not bedbugs.

"Tina, bring the milk."

Mrs. Manayan's daughter walked across the room delicately balancing the full glass of milk on her hand. After childhood, Mai Lan had never gulped down a full glass of milk.

"Nurse, please. This for you."

Mrs. Manayan was a Samoan woman married to a Filipino man. Her pidgin English and Mai Lan's imitation of it were enough for them to negotiate a mutual understanding. Looking at the glass of milk, Mai Lan remembered the Bible verse from the morning. *"I fed you with milk, not solid food."*

Mai Lan couldn't very well refuse since this was her very first encounter with the lady. Her head swam after she gulped the milk. Enough of her thinking was left, though, for her to go over the reason for her visit. After listening to Mai Lan, Mrs. Manayan looked shocked.

"You mean the *ukus* all over the floor? The pillows, the beds, everywhere? You mean I have to shampoo them all one time? And wash everything? You crazy or what?"

Crazy or not, Mai Lan's mission was to convince Mrs. Manayan that, indeed, her kids couldn't return to school unless they were free of lice.

Mrs. Manayan looked at Mai Lan with round incredulous eyes. Mai Lan looked into her wide- open pupils and felt like she had to stay with Mrs Manayan and do the work herself.

"Mrs. Manayan, I know it's impossible work to do, but you get Tina to help. Get your husband to help too."

Visions of dancing *ukus* crept into Mai Lan's head. "Can you take the mats outside and brush them with soap and water and let the sun dry them? And put all the beddings and clothes through the washer and dryer? And make the water as hot as you can, also the dryer as hot as you can?"

Mrs. Manayan's eyes softened somewhat, but she still remained speechless. "Here, I give you these bottles of shampoo and fine-tooth combs. You shampoo everybody's head all one time same day, then comb out all the *uku* eggs."

Mrs. Manayan held her hands out, grabbed the bottles, then looked at them, turned them round and round while Mai Lan spelled out instructions how to use them. The look of disgust on her face remained all throughout Mai Lan's talk.

"Mrs. Manayan, I come back next week to see how else I can help you. Thank you for being so nice to me."

The week after, Mai Lan decided to take Malia with her for visits to two families in the valley, in addition to checking on Mrs. Manayan. Mai Lan thought it should be interesting for her daughter to witness some of her work and, she hoped, to see the beauty of it. Malia undoubtedly only saw one aspect of life when she followed her father to his office or mingled with her friends in private school. This experience of seeing how people live at the edge should hopefully stir some compassion in her.

Say waited for them in front of the apartment.

"Say, my daughter Malia."

Say lifted her head and squinted her unseeing eyes toward Mai Lan's voice. Mai Lan put Malia's hand in Say's.

"Say, my daughter Malia. She come for visit."

"Hi, Malia."

"Hi, Say."

"How's school, Say? Someone help you get your food at lunch?"

"Oh yes, nurse, my friends help me."

"Who taking you to Dr. Mark for checkups?"

"My dad."

"Where's Dad? He in the house?"

"No. He working."

"I give you this paper. You give Dad. It has dates for shots to keep you well. You ask him take you to clinic, okay?"

Mai Lan watched her daughter and Say holding hands. Malia had a nice smile on her lips, so did Say. Mai Lan will ask her daughter for her impressions of Palolo Valley Homes on their way home.

They headed toward the next housing unit. No one waited for them there. The apartment occupant's barely audible voice greeted them when they pushed open the front door. The lights were not on despite the darkness inside. The old lady was in bed. Empty liquor bottles littered the floor. Malia stayed quietly by the door. Mai Lan started checking her patient's pulse and got her blood- pressure apparatus out. The woman's pulse was regular and strong. Mai Lan hoped her blood pressure would be within normal limits.

Wham! The front door opened violently. Minh appeared, grabbed Malia's arm, and pulled her out in a hurry. "Come home, what are you doing here?"

Mai Lan stared in disbelief. She started shaking but steadied herself.

Oh, God, what's happening? What do I do now? How can he do such a thing? He's been following me?

"She is just tagging along so she can see what I do as a nurse. Is there something wrong with that?"

"This is no place for her to be."

Then they left. Sometime after that event, Minh asked her to help one acquaintance of his in the community who was hospitalized for a nervous breakdown because of worries about her family in Vietnam. Mai Lan could hear the young girl sobbing in the background. It was her turn to retaliate.

"No, no help from me, dear husband. You can go to hell with your friend."

Bewildered, Malia got quieter as time went by. Many times, Mai Lan found her sitting on the high shelf of the closet in her bedroom, talking to her imaginary friends. Mike was in his early teenage years and hung around his friends after school. He practically disappeared from her life. One day, she came home from work and found both kids in front of the house, playing with matches and lighting fires inside several empty cans.

Other than that, life continued with the usual routines.

CHAPTER 8

Mai Lan's World

Let no one separate them, for God has joined them together.
—Mark 10:9

The storm would only last for one day. Justin of Channel 2 said so. Mai Lan didn't know about his predictions. He looked very self-assured broadcasting on TV, but her past experience told her that God played with him half of the time. When he said it would rain, God made the weather beautiful and so on. In any case, this time, she woke up to gray skies. Fine raindrops started sprinkling the whole island by early afternoon. It looked like nighttime by four o'clock. She served dinner at five o'clock. Minh's parents joined them that day.

Mother sat down at the table, lifted her empty bowl to her eyebrows, and murmured to herself a few words of thanks to Buddha. Then she poked her chopsticks right down the placemat, holding on firmly to keep them upright while digging into the table, looked around at the spread of food, and asked Mai Lan, "Why is there nothing to eat?"

Mai Lan had spent the whole day cooking a total of five dishes. The rice—of course, no decent meal could go without rice—plus a sweet-and-sour soup of fish, pineapple, bean sprouts, tomatoes, and various herbs; then a veggie stew in soy sauce; a stir-fry of swamp cabbage; and a small bowl of dipping sauce for the fish in the soup.

The kids squirmed in their seats. Her husband looked at the ceiling. She wanted to melt into the ground. She had no reply. She couldn't think of any retort. It was no small feat to put together a complete Vietnamese meal in the middle of childcare, clean the home, work at the hospital, shop, drive, and everything else in between. Mai Lan left the table and went to work in the kitchen.

Outside, the rain splashed onto the grass, creating puddles that grew by the minute. It tapped on the roof with little fingers of sounds, which earlier seemed like notes of joy in a familiar song from her childhood, but now grew into thundering notes of anger. She banged the pots and pans around. The kitchen sank into a blur of gray with flashes of red shooting through from time to time.

The dark night suddenly looked like a heaven of calm in spite of the rain. Inside her was a perfect match for the storm outside. That was where she belonged—in that night with that storm. She ran outside and walked through the neighborhood.

She plunged into the dark space with delight. In that rain, Corky started dancing in front of her. He had gradually come into her life over the last several months. With Corky came wonderment, a lot of fears, and also much relief from the anguish at how her marriage was going. At first, she thought he was a product of her imagination, but then she knew herself well enough to know that her brain would not invent a character as complex as Corky.

In the rain, she watched him draw graceful swirls in gold and silver ahead of her.

She jogged partly, walked partly, with the water sloshing around her ankles and her slippers pounding a rhythmical beat. The water was dancing around her; the water wrapped her in its embrace. It submerged her in a wonderful cold stream. It soothed her soul and showed her the joy of another world—a world of darkness, a strange world of inner struggles, dominated by an entity known only to her.

Life had been a daily struggle for quite a while. She dragged herself out of bed in the morning and crashed with exhaustion at the end of the day. Sleep was anything but restful. About midnight, her eyes exploded with events. They came like dreams etched on a gray background, dreams of fluid, hazy forms floating and changing from one shape to another. Then from one night to the next, they slowly took on colors, seemingly springing from the mud into dancing worm shapes, colors that looked dull and nauseating, but that gradually morphed into sharp lines shooting in an explosion of all shades of the rainbow.

The lines danced as if in a symphony that a divine hand had drawn across her eyelids. They curved, twisted, shot straight, then curved again in multicolored arabesques. They intertwined, then untangled. They straightened and then interlocked; they zigzagged, thickened, then thinned out. They kept her tossing and turning around. They were entertaining enough, if only she could shake the fear of all these lines scratching her eyes and making her go blind.

Opening her eyes in the morning, she let out a sigh of relief after looking at the ceiling, the walls, and the pictures. Comparing distance, details, and colors, she came to the conclusion that her eyesight had not suffered. She wished the show would cease so she could have her sleep back intact, but day in and out, it continued.

One day, after dancing their arabesques, the lines gracefully curved and formed a word with many colors in cursive font—*Corky*.

The word *corky* is used for an object much like the cork on top of a wine bottle. It's a screw that can twist inside the body, be it on the surface or deep in the internal organs. It has the shape of a question mark, and anywhere the point of the question mark enters the body, it leaves pain. Much greater than pain, though, was when Corky decided to use the Chinese feather touch. At least, that's how Mai Lan felt. The Chinese invented this form of torture when they used a light feather to tickle the soles of the enemies' feet repeatedly until the nerves were raw. She obviously didn't know how much information was obtained to help the Chinese get what they wanted, but if Corky kept it up, she would go bonkers. Luckily, he would tease her and then stop. She hated the game because as soon as Corky started gyrating inside her ears, nose, eyes, or anywhere else, it seemed like worms were crawling there. The sensations triggered unbearable pain and scorched her brain raw. If she was doing the dishes, she would tear the gloves off. If she was steering the wheel of the car, she would swerve. If she was in bed, she would jump to her feet. The worms only stopped crawling when her hand was massaging the area. Inside the ears or the nose, she would thrust her finger in. On the eyeballs, she would massage them or part the eyelids with both fingers to ease the pain. With other parts of the body, she would put her hands under her clothes and scratch, pinch, pull, or knead until Corky let go.

Most of the time, he didn't stay long. He would screw, then let go. In the silence that followed his departure, she tried all her might to soothe out his mean touch. At times, he would put a stop to her madness by insisting—"You're gonna have holes in your skin" or "Stop it. It's not me. Don't blame it on me. Don't you see the devil at work?"

*****

In the calm after the storm, she invariably went over what mistake was made that day. If she couldn't uncover any to mull over, she would review all the misdeeds of the past and lament on her suffering.

One day, out of desperation, she decided to try something new. She turned to Jesus and asked for protection, "Jesus, please deliver me from evil, protect me and guide me. Let your blood cover my sins and lead me to a better life."

Suzanne was the person who introduced to her the idea that there is God who oversees this whole world and that He sent His Son, Jesus, to die on the cross for the sins of those who believe in Him. Suzanne lived in Mai Lan's neighborhood, and their kids went to the same school. Mai Lan had learned much from Suzanne, who readily helped when help was needed. By then, Minh and Mai Lan had lived many years away from their old country but were still not fully integrated into the local society.

Gradually, Mai Lan learned of God who is the creator of the universe, not like Buddha, who is a prince born of a king and queen in India. She was amazed that God's son was born in a stable, grew up poor, and led a life of no sin. Comparing the lives of Jesus and Buddha, she realized that Buddha was indeed a human being just like her, though much richer and more powerful, and that he sinned like everyone else. How could he just leave his wife and child and disappear into the night to seek wisdom without a word of warning or a goodbye? Did he care about his wife and son?

On a beautiful morning, Suzanne brought her Bible with a few written words from a Vietnamese pastor.

"Mai Lan, you will not believe what I am going to tell you. Look at this writing and tell me what it says."

With disbelief, Mai Lan read the words written in Vietnamese addressed to her: "Mrs Nguyen, please accept this Bible with the Lord's blessings. He will be with you for the rest of your life and beyond." Mai Lan recognized by the signature the founding pastor of the first Vietnamese Mennonite church in Honolulu. She then asked, "Suzanne, how in the world did you get this Bible? This pastor does not know me. I never attended this church."

"That's why I told you, you will not believe this story. Sit down and listen. Last year, my husband was in a Bible class at the Bible insti-tute. The man sitting next to Roland is the pastor of the Vietnamese Mennonite church. Of course, they got acquainted, and one day, the pastor gave him this Bible with instructions to keep it until the time comes to give it to you. So we kept it in our bookcase, all the while wondering what this is all about. Look at the date the pastor wrote you these words. Do you know what today's date is?"

Mai Lan's eyes almost popped out of their sockets. Today was exactly one year after the date written in the Bible.

Suzanne waited patiently for a possible explanation to this most unusual event.

It came after a while: "You know, this pastor must have heard of Minh's suicide and prayed for me to know that God exists and is standing by to help. I thank you and Roland for keeping it so faithfully."

It took Mai Lan almost one year to finish reading the Bible in its entirety. She kept looking for where Jesus committed sin like Buddha or anyone of us human beings. She couldn't find any.

She was so desperate for relief from Corky that she called on Jesus. If He really was the Son of God, He should be able to help. And it worked!

Corky, would you please leave me alone and not torture me anymore?

It was pretty incredible, but after that request, the little corks in the shape of question marks, which had caused so much pain, physical as well as emotional, disappeared completely.

Corky, however, remained. He remained as a friend. It seemed like whenever she was in a bind, he was there. Most of the time, he had questions for her to get her brain focusing on what to do; other times, he would provide the answer right away. There were times, too, when she would seek an answer and get only a deafening silence.

Tonight, in the middle of the storm, Corky's reply was totally upsetting to Mai Lan: "Why are you so upset? You know Mother. That's how she is. What do you think? She will praise your cooking? She will pity you for the time you spent in the kitchen?"

Mai Lan started laughing. How stupid of her! Then she asked Corky, "So I can't talk back to her. How am I to go on living with her?"

Corky went on drawing his arabesques in the darkness.

"Remember, she managed to have her elder daughter accept two betrothal gifts at the same time, and her younger daughter was engaged to one guy and married another. Why should it be different for your husband and you? Why should you be happy together and not split?"

"Maybe I can move somewhere with the kids. Get a divorce or something. Leave that stupid husband of mine and get a life."

Corky suddenly yelled into her ears, "You are not going to do anything like that!" Then he disappeared into the night.

*****

The rain poured buckets of water all over the neighborhood. The wind howled and hurled glacial blows at her body. Then God thundered across the sky with flashes of repeated lightnings.

Silhouettes of trees and houses loomed over her, engulfed her spirit in awe and fear at the same time, then disappeared into the darkness. She swerved and turned and bent, trying to stand up, but ended up bending almost to the ground. Slowly, she made her way back to the house, drenched to the bone.

The day after, the news showed the bus stop at the entrance to her neighborhood. The big yellow poinciana tree had toppled on its side in the thunderstorm, fallen on the roof of the bus stop, and split it in half. Debris was strewn all over the street.

Mai Lan shuddered. Her Vietnamese middle name translated to "yellow poinciana." *Did God want to strike me out?* she wondered. *Who am I that He would strike the yellow poinciana at the bus stop to warn me?*

CHAPTER 9

The Spy

I went down to the nut orchard
To look at the blossoms of the valley
To see whether the vines had budded
Whether the pomegranates were in bloom
Before I was aware, my desire set me
Among the chariots of my kinsman, a prince.
—Song of Solomon 6:11–12

Mai Lan's world grew more and more chaotic with each passing day. How could life continue this way? Inside her was a tug-of-war.

Minh was still her husband, but he was now a stranger. She could recall the lover of the times when they first met, then the doting father who spoiled their two kids. Now it was more like he wanted them all to himself and vied with her on who was to have the most say in how to raise them.

One day, Mike handed Mai Lan a note from the school. "Minh, what do you think of this? Which second language do you want our son to choose when he gets to the next grade? How should I respond?"

"Put in French."

"We live in Hawaii. Shouldn't we have him learn Japanese? It's more practical."

"Mai Lan, French is part of our heritage. Put down French."

So French it would be.

Mai Lan had a heated talk with Mother-in-Law about how unbearable the situation had become for her and Minh. "Mother, God made husband and wife and said that a man shall leave his father and mother and hold fast to his wife, and they shall become one flesh. As far as I can tell, your son is not paying attention to his wife at all. He spends his time with you at your place, he is hardly home. Our family must follow all his dictates. I have no say whatever in the running of my own household."

"Mai Lan, don't you see that a son who is good to his mother and father will also be good to his wife? Just estimate yourself lucky that you have such a husband."

Mai Lan would have more luck banging her head into a wall. She made no further attempt at trying to change the old lady's mind. Solace came from the workplace.

"Mai Lan, you've got to meet the new resident from med school. He's a hit."

Indeed he was nice-looking except for his bald head. He had eyes as blue as the sky, a square jaw like John Wayne's, and a welcoming smile. His stroll was always easy in spite of the hectic pace at the clinic. Mai Lan fell for him the minute she saw him.

In the mornings as she got ready for the day's work, Minh started noticing more makeup on her face and new tighter-fitting uniforms. Work had become very distracting for Mai Lan. She walked around the house in a trance. *I want to be with him. I'll walk the white sands of Waikiki in his arms under the moonlight. I'll dance in his embrace. He will sweep me off my feet into a dream world, and we will be happy forever. Like in the fairy tales.*

Meanwhile, Minh had become a beloved leader of the Vietnamese community. His name was on all the refugees' lips. He was called upon to resolve challenges of resettlement between them and the state of Hawaii. He was present at almost all community events as the motivational speaker. Invitations to weddings, funerals, anniversaries of deaths, and even birthdays came regularly, and he attended these alone. His reputation spread beyond Hawaii, and he received invitations to speak in other states then other countries. Awards recognized his services and accomplishments.

How can I win against such prestige? Suppose I file for divorce. Which judge in this whole wide world would give me my kids? I cannot live without my kids. Oh, God, how can I continue on? Oh that my prince would come to the rescue!

And voila! Fate intervened. Next week she would fly to Maui with several other staff members to help in the establishment of a new clinic. And guess what? The resident would be part of the crew!

Minh took her to the airport. *Why in the world does she have all that makeup on? Look at that blissful expression! What a whore!*

Maui was the perfect setting for romance. They stayed at a small hotel in the countryside near Kahului. Daytime was busy with setting up the clinic. At nighttime, the group met to plan for the next day's work.

Mai Lan looked for the right time to make a move. She had a burning desire to fall into the resident's arms. At the same time, a feeling of dread followed her in the form of a bee, of all things. The bee had been following her everywhere she went. The bee waited for her in the morning when she stepped out of her hotel room, buzzed at her side when she ate breakfast, flew into the clinic rooms, and settled on the ceiling during work hours. When she tried to get closer to her prince, it circled around them.

Have you ever tried to kiss somebody with a bee buzzing around you? When Mai Lan saw Minh again at the airport, she felt like she was drowning. Nothing happened in Maui. Nothing but a stupid bee following her around.

Fate did not stop there. Several weeks later, Mai Lan received an invitation. Her prince would have a party at his abode, and she was invited. Alleluia! There was a picture of him on the invitation, and he looked rather unusual—he had makeup on and earrings dangled from his ears.

What the heck! I'll go and find out.

The house was swimming in purple decorations. The scent of incense floated all around, the punch bowl billowed out white smoke, and the food was laden with Middle East spices. Many guests were swathed in saris. Some of them wore only T-shirts, which showed bodybuilders' arms. One of them even got down on the floor and started writhing toward Mai Lan. She suddenly had visions of soldiers fighting the Vietnam War. Mai Lan had never attended a more exotic party nor been in a stranger environment.

She said goodbye to the resident in a hurry. The prince had morphed into a princess who was surrounded with drugs. The bee buzzing around her in Maui had been sent from heaven.

*****

This afternoon was just like any other afternoon. Home from work, Mai Lan headed straight for the kitchen.

"What's that on the table?" she said to herself. She grabbed the letter. "Something Minh wants me to do?"

No, the letter was from Vietnam, sent a long time ago. It had been stored in her closet along with other correspondence from her relatives and friends. How did it end up here on the table?

Shortly after the war ended, her cousin from the north got in touch. Uncle Number Three was in the north during the war, had married, and had a daughter. The letter described horrible scenes of destruction because of the rains of fire from American bombs. It also spoke of wanting to know the cousin she had never met.

Mai Lan decided she was not in the right frame of mind to carry on with a relative, especially one from the north, and stuck the letter in the closet.

How in the world did it end up on this table? A handyman was recently engaged and had the run of the house when no one was home. With parents working and kids in school, did he get nosy? As far as Mai Lan could tell, nothing was missing or misplaced. But why, if it was him, would he single out this letter?

Or had someone decided to dig in their past? Minh was now well-known in the refugee community. Was it a threat from Commie agents, a question from the FBI or CIA, or just Minh leaving the damn letter on the table?

Minh could not explain the mystery. He had ties to the Vietcong, too, through his ex-girlfriend and his family, as did many other families during the war.

He is lucky he got married to me. Had he proceeded with the secretary at the New Zealand Embassy, she would have gotten him in deep trouble. Who knows? By now, he would have stolen information from all his contacts in the government and sent them to the Commies. Don't you think it's a possibility?

In any case, aside from this letter from her cousin, there was another letter, which Auntie Number Six sent when she first set foot on this land of the free and the brave, asking her to send back tanning lotion for the comrades buried in the underground of Cu Chi. They needed the lotion so they could appear as peasants tilling the soil instead of moles that have not seen the sun in ages.

Mai Lan did not respond to the letter. Rather, she threw it away and forgot about it. Now that the mystery of why Cousin's letter ended on the dining table started haunting her, she wondered what kind of karma was following Minh and her around.

She began noticing cars following her with cameras pointed at her. In the parking lots at the shopping centers, along the streets as she entered or exited the clinics, they popped up everywhere. One of the cars that followed Mai Lan regularly ended up in the neighborhood.

*****

Finally, I will get to know the truth! Mai Lan grabbed the letter from the mailbox, opened it in a hurry, and pored over the contents. This letter was not from Vietnam, but was something Minh and she had sought.

Minh had noticed the obvious changes in Mai Lan's behavior and decided to contact a private investigation agency for help. On pins and needles, Mai Lan had waited for the results of their inquiries into the people who followed her.

"As far as what can be determined, there are no listening devices on the premises of your residence at this time. This would include wire intrusions between the telephone at your residence and the telephone-switching station. It would appear that the telephone or other lines are not being used to convey signals to or from microphones in your residence. There does not appear to be any evidence of authorized shortwave radio transmissions from the residence. While we cannot guarantee that this has always been the case, we found no evidence of intrusion in the past.

"Concerning the auto you suspect of causing harassment to you and family, the license number is registered to Derek and Grace Brown, who reside at 567 Wild Street. They have resided at this address for a number of years. A map is enclosed showing the location."

Mai Lan stared at the map. It showed a place on the other side of the island. There was an area circled in red, the middle of which was the address referred to.

"You stated when we met you that the above names were not familiar to you. As far as we are concerned, our investigation into their background reveals no reason to suspect that either of them would have reason to have any interest in you, your husband, family, etc. In fact, I am almost sure that they are not aware of your identity. They seem to have friends in your locality, and that probability is the reason they were there when you spotted them. You may have seen them since or you may do so in the future.

"We have now completed our check of outside agencies. As far as we can determine, there should be no cause for alarm, and neither you nor your husband is under suspicion by the following named agencies. You are, of course, on record with some of those agencies, but the record is normal as can be with none of them showing the cause for suspicion of you or your activities. Due to the coverage these agencies are involved in, I would also presume that they would be aware should an agency of a foreign power be attempting to harass you or bring your name or sympathies into ill repute or attempt to intrude upon your privacy.

"Such agencies would include those on a local level such as the Honolulu Police Department; Honolulu City and County agencies, such as the drug enforcement office of the prosecutor; State of Hawaii through various agencies, including the attorney general; and

US federal government, such as the Department of Labor, Federal Bureau of Investigation, Central Intelligence Agency, Immigration and Naturalization Service, US Treasury Department (Secret Service), Department of Defense, Drug Enforcement Administration of the Department of Justice, US Army, Navy, Air Force Intelligence, National Aeronautics and Space Administration, and US Department of Health, Education, and Welfare."

Mai Lan stared at the letter in disbelief. Her head began to swim.

How in the world did the letter from the cousin land on the dining table?

CHAPTER 10

Is There God?

Be still, and know that I am God.

—Psalms 46:10

"It's time we take a vacation."

They packed up and headed for Little Saigon in Westminster. Little Saigon is the largest Vietnamese community in the US. It's brimming with food not found outside of Vietnam.

Mai Lan was amazed that its main street, Bolsa Avenue, had only shopping malls, restaurants, and supermarkets all adorned with Vietnamese names exclusively. One could live here and speak Vietnamese and ignore the rest of America for the remainder of one's life.

Minh delighted in towing the family around to sample Vietnamese food from pho to banh mi to other delicacies, especially specialties coming from various areas of Vietnam.

"Dad, what are those statues for?"

"Oh! They represent luck, prosperity, and longevity. Much of our culture has its origin in Chinese culture, and people use these symbols all the time to wish each other the best things in life." They took pictures of the giant statues in front of the most famous landmark of Little Saigon.

They also visited the statues of Vietnamese and American soldiers standing in solidarity, a commemoration of the war that happened not too long ago. Flowers were regularly placed in front of them. This Vietnamese community would not be here without that war.

Alas! Any escape from the humdrum of daily life must come to an end. They had to leave Westminster and go back to Honolulu.

Minh unlocked the front door and pushed the suitcases in. All was calm and orderly, exactly as it was before they left. Then it hit them.

"What's that smell?"

It was an odd, nauseating sweet but foul odor of putrefaction, which invaded the nostrils—subtle at first, then installing itself and staying put. Mai Lan turned around. The trash can was full of dried maggots nesting in the middle of rotten apple cores and streaks of hardened brown liquid. Some of the maggots streamed out of the trash can onto the floor. It was a scene of awful rotted organic material, the source of that horrible smell. She thought the house was left in order. But, of course, not. It had been fourteen days that this trash had been festering. She shuddered at the vision of maggots crawling all over their living space those fourteen days.

The kids retreated into the yard. Minh and Mai Lan sprang into action. In a hurry, Mai Lan opened the kitchen cabinets, pulled out gloves, Clorox, wipes, and bags. Together, they got on their knees and scrubbed. The whole mess found its proper place outside the house in the big trash bin.

Minh went to get the kids. Instead of getting a much-needed rest, Mai Lan opened the suitcases and dumped some dirty clothes into the washing machine. She started pouring the liquid detergent into the washer. Her elbow hit the corner of the washer and a jet of detergent hit the carpet. Now she had to clean this too.

The devil must be residing in this house. Have you ever tried to scrub a carpet clean of a thick viscous liquid that clings like tar? *This must be my punishment for being away and having a good time. Cleaning, cleaning, and cleaning. Devil, what is the next cleaning to be done?*

She hurried to the closet, fumbled around. Digging for the washcloths, she pulled out a beautiful towel embroidered with a manger scene. *Aha! I will use this towel to wipe up all the detergent. Never mind Christmas. Christmas does not exist.*

She filled a bucket with water, hurried back to the washer, got on her knees, and started scrubbing. It took tons of water to remove the sticky stuff, as well as muscle power, concentration, and mechanical thinking. Kind of like a mantra in motion that calms the mind and gradually displaces the panic that seemed to have descended lately and whisper into her ears that the whole world had come down on her. Exhausted, she finally gave up the scrubbing. Finishing the job would have to wait until tomorrow.

Back to the kitchen, the smell of dead flesh still hung in the air, though it was subtler now. The liquefied mass of feed for germs, along with the maggots, was gone. Mai Lan's throat felt like sawdust. With her head spinning slightly in a whirlwind of black and white, she opened the cabinet, looking for a glass. Lining the edge of the cabinet were gray and black spots. This time, it was not maggots. They were dead flies.

Mai Lan ran out the door and screamed.

At that instant, a car parked across the street roared up like thunder, swerved around like a cockroach hit by a stream of pest killer, grazed a car parked in the next block, took out its front bumper, then disappeared around the corner. Mai Lan's heart almost stopped. Here they were again—the spies. In spite of what the letter from the investigative agency said, the spies were back.

Next day, on the way back from the supermarket, Mai Lan stooped slightly in the car to rearrange the shopping bags on the floor of the passenger side. It was pretty dark in the garage. It seemed like the darkness intensified for a few seconds, then the world started turning a bit. A vague feeling, or was it fear, grew in her, warning of nausea coming. She stiffened, thought of becoming a twig, shut her eyes for a few seconds, then straightened her body slowly to draw back into the driver seat to take a deep breath and relax her muscles. Keeping her eyes shut, she tried to empty all thoughts from her mind. The dizziness seemed to leave.

She eased herself out of the seat. A whirlwind sensation rocked slightly just like gentle waves on a calm sea, then gave way to solid ground. The sensation returned a couple times while Mai Lan froze herself and waited.

Devil, leave me alone. Go away. Go. How do I retrieve all these grocery bags and carry them to the kitchen?

She slowly opened the door, eased herself out, then put her hands on the car's body to slowly make her way to the passenger side. The same rocking motion took over when she bent down to lift the bags. Shutting her eyes halfway, with one hand clutching the grocery bag and the other sticking out to the front, Mai Lan put one foot in front of the other, then step by step headed to the front door of the house, unlocked it, and put the bag down.

"Wow, I did it!" *Keep your eyes shut! Keep them shut!*

She got back to the car for the second bag.

When she finally lowered herself onto the couch, sitting erect for a moment, then sinking into the pillows, the dizziness disappeared.

Wow! It feels like heaven now. God is definitely here. "Be still, and know that I am God." *The devil is gone.* Mai Lan realized that whatever was happening to her ranged from the unusual to the eerie. Her life now had turned into moments of trying to control successive events that happened for no reason. And they happened so fast that she didn't get any reprieve.

I am not sharing any of these weird thoughts about spies, the devil, and God. People will think I am crazy, and I am not.

So she kept mum and carried on as best she could. About a week after the dizziness episode, she headed for the shopping center in a suburb by the sea.

On this beautiful morning, sunrays flooded the marina, and the breeze rustled the hibiscus hedges lining the streets. Deciding she had some time to wander around for a bit before getting back into her routine, she stopped at one of the side streets to admire a plumeria tree laden with pink flowers.

Across the street, a big rig suddenly revved up, then seemed to aim at her. Mai Lan's eyes widened with terror. However, the rig did not seem to be able to make up its mind on what to do. It kept on moving back and forth in small jerks, as if it wanted to come at her but was held back by a strength it could not overcome.

Suddenly the whole neighborhood came alive. A helicopter appeared out of nowhere. Its engine grew louder and louder until it boomed in her ears. It whirled around back and forth, flying lower and lower, until it spewed out contingents of soldiers in fighting gear, each holding a rifle pointed at her.

Then ignoring her, the soldiers started scaling the walls of the houses in the subdivision all around her. Strangely enough, when they reached the rooftops, they slid back to the bottoms and went back up again. Mai Lan got dizzy looking at them. She thought of scenes in a movie. But this was no movie. And this was Hawaii, which had no war whatsoever. Turning around, she ran to the car.

These visions kept coming. On a trip to Chinatown, there would be Buddhist monks in saffron robes following her. To check it out, she sat on a low wall on a street to see what they would do. They tried to hide in the bushes on the other side of the street. She walked again. They walked too. She stopped. They stopped. Her heart pounded. Her hands were wet with sweat.

Time went by. She learned to stay home. The daily routine of cleaning, cooking, and taking care of the children kept her going. She suppressed all feelings and stopped all conversations. She just put food on the table for Minh and the kids and shut herself in the bedroom.

*****

They started counselling with Dr. Stein. Minh took her to his office once a week with the two kids in tow. While Mike and Malia stayed in the waiting room, they tried to find a way out of this maze. In the office of the psychiatrist, Mai Lan found a safe place to unburden herself of all her hatred of Mother-in-Law. As for Minh, he did not utter one word the whole time. His duty was to take her there in the hope of getting back his wife.

Several weeks into counselling, Dr. Stein asked them to take a personality test. The Myers-Briggs Type Indicator assessments came back—both of them were the introverted types.

However, she had a perceptive attitude while he had more of a judging tendency. Mai Lan pored over her description with fascination. It was just like looking in the mirror and seeing herself for the first time.

This sort of person had as much wealth of feeling as the extrovert but used it differently. He cared more deeply about fewer things. He was warm inside, like a fur-lined coat. It did not show until you got past his reserve. He also had a strong loyalty to duty and obligations, but he chose his final values without reference to outsiders and stuck to them with passionate conviction. Though he found them hard to talk about, these inner loyalties and ideals governed his life.

He was tolerant, open-minded, understanding, flexible, and adaptable, though when one of his inner loyalties were threatened, he would not give an inch. Except for work's sake, he had little wish to impress or dominate. The contacts he prized were with people who understood his values.

He was twice as good when working at a job he believed in because his feelings put added steam behind his efforts. He wanted his work to contribute to something that mattered—perhaps to human understanding or health or happiness or maybe to the perfecting of some product or undertaking. He wanted a purpose behind his paycheck, no matter the amount of the check. He was a perfectionist concerning feelings and usually happiest at individual work involving personal values. With high ability, he could be good in literature, art, science, or psychology.

This type's special problem was that he might feel so marked a contrast between his inner ideals and outer reality as to burden himself with a sense of inadequacy. If his ideals had no channel of expression, they made him too vulnerable, affecting his confidence in life and in himself.

Wow! Maybe that's why she imagined all those scenes of chaos, conflicts, and fantastic pursuits with soldiers, moving trucks, and Buddhist monks rather than face the reality of her miserable life. Maybe her ideas of child-rearing required some way of being realized rather than always yielding to the dictates of her husband and mother-in-law.

More fascination came with reading about Minh and how he viewed the world.

This introverted intuitive was the innovator in the field of ideas, principles, and systems of thought. He trusted his intuitive insight as to the true relationships and meanings of things, regardless of established authority or popularly accepted beliefs. Further, he had faith in his inner vision of the possibility that he could remove mountains and often did. In the process, he might drive or oppose others as hard as he drove himself. Problems only stimulated him. He believed that the impossible takes a little longer but not much.

He backed up his original insights with determination, perseverance, and enduring purpose. He wanted his ideas worked out in practice, applied, and accepted and would spend time and effort necessary to reach that end.

The danger for this type arose from his single-minded focus. He saw his goal so clearly that he might miss other things that he should see, even though they conflicted with that goal—the rights, interests, feelings, and points of view of other people and the facts, conditions, and counterforces that exist and must be reckoned with. He needed to talk over his plans with an extroverted person and really listen.

He was outstandingly effective in scientific research and design engineering where his bold and ingenious ideas had to meet and fit with reality. He would always need some, such as reality check, but the very boldness of his ideas could be of immense value in any field and should not be smothered in a routine job.

If his judgment was undeveloped, he could neither listen to outside judgment nor criticize his own inner vision.

Mai Lan was stunned. With such a personality as what Minh had, how could she persuade him to change and allow her more decision-making in the marriage? She had tried to adapt to being second-class citizen and cater to everyone. Mother-in-Law still pulled her strings behind the scene, and Minh still gave due consideration to her wishes. All these years, except for when they began their marriage, Mai Lan had felt smothered by Minh and his mother.

The psychiatrist suggested that Mother come to some of the sessions, but she refused. Mai Lan wouldn't be surprised if she was of the same type of personality as her son.

So week after week, she unburdened herself of the emotional load that put a stone in her chest and fantastic visions in her mind. She recalled all the indignities suffered at Mother's hands that she had kept hidden from her husband. She poured out her frustrations and outrage.

The strangest thing was that Minh just sat there in Dr. Stein's office and listened to her without uttering a word, and the doctor also kept quiet, sometimes even turning his back to them to look at the wall behind his desk.

Slowly, the stone lifted off her chest, and the horrors of people spying on her disappeared. She now saw more clearly the situation she was faced with, but Minh's personality had not changed. He still was a powerful representative of the refugee community, the head of the family, and the breadwinner now—the sole breadwinner because she had lost her ability to earn money after all the extraordinary delusions invaded her mind.

Mai Lan, first things first. Go find money so that you can be independent.

She got back into nursing, then went to see a lawyer. "Minh, I want a divorce. My lawyer will send you a letter soon."

CHAPTER 11

The Day He Left

Fall seasons coming one by one with changing leaves
Leaves falling and covering the grave of our love
Leaves flying yet heavy with our passing lives
Thinking of you, I fill this glass.

Minh lifted the cup of guava juice from the table, then turning to Mai Lan, nodded to her, and put the cup to his lips.

His suitcase was ready. Tomorrow, his cousin would come pick him up and drive him to his parents' apartment so he could have some company and, she hoped, recover from his despondency. His life had gone downhill fast ever since she announced she wanted a divorce. Now he would be with his parents for a while instead of waiting all day for his wife and kids to come back home in the evening. At least, that's what Mai Lan hoped for—a change in scenery for him.

*****

"What a beautiful baby! She weighs thirteen pounds, just right for her age. What are you giving her that makes her grow so fast?"

Mai Lan beamed at the mom while picking the baby up from the scale. Suddenly, the door to the exam room opened.

"Mai Lan, they want you in the office. I'll take over."

The other nurse on the team took the baby out of Mai Lan's arms, then waved her out.

"Here, dear, someone wants to talk to you."

The clerk handed the phone to her, then stood by, waiting.

"Cousin, cousin, your husband jumped from the lanai."

A series of sobs burst through the receiver. Mai Lan tried to understand. Her cousin-in-law must have gone crazy. *Why is she sobbing so much? It must be someone she knows who jumped from a lanai. Who could that be? Why is she calling me? She knows I am working."*

The sobs kept coming.

All of a sudden, a dark curtain fell over Mai Lan's eyes. She swayed onto the clerk's chest, grabbed her arms, and sank halfway to the floor. The clerk planted her squarely on a nearby chair, then picked up the phone.

Time grew longer and longer. Finally, Mai Lan asked for the phone. "Cousin, what happened?"

"We took your husband to his parents and left him there with his father. The rest of us, including your mother, went shopping. Then we came back. Your father was sitting on the couch in the living room, but we couldn't find your husband anywhere. We looked all over the apartment, couldn't find him. Looked again, no result. We finally went down to the building office to ask if anyone had seen him. That's when they told us someone jumped from the lanai onto the parking lot. Oh, cousin, I am sorry. I am so sorry."

Mai Lan handed the phone back to the clerk. Her head buzzed. Her whole body shook. She stared straight ahead blindly. Time stretched out to eternity. She just sat, not thinking. *There is no past, no future. No world, no people, nothing. Just a blank wall. That's it, the world is a blank wall. No, make it that we get there as soon as we can. No, he is still alive. This can't be. He didn't jump. Someone else did, not him.*

Those thoughts rolled over just like a recording in her head—one by one, nonstop. When they stopped for a few seconds, a blank canvas fell in front of her eyes. Then the thoughts took over again. Then she felt a presence at her sides. Her boss took over.

"Mai Lan, two nurses who work regularly with you will take you to where your husband is in your own car. They will come back to the clinic after that. They already have your purse and your lunchbox. Do you feel you can go now?"

Mai Lan stared at the boss, then stood up and followed her coworkers.

The ride to his parents' apartment was completely silent. Part of her wanted to fly as fast as she could; the other part wanted time to stop and roll back to when they were together the night before. A policewoman stood at the entrance to the parking lot. As soon as the car was parked in the guest stall, she grabbed Mai Lan's hands and led her to the building office then to an inside room. Mother was there, sitting in an armchair, eyes closed, hands slowly stringing beads from her Buddhist amulet while she softly recited her mantra. A few people were in the room. The police started asking questions. Mai Lan answered as best as she could.

"What happened? When did you last see him? When did you go to work? Who brought him to this building?"

"Where is my husband? Can I see him?"

"Sorry, we'll take you to him now. He is covered with a sheet. Don't come too close. But you can stand nearby and be with him in that way."

The officer took Mai Lan by the gate separating the parking lot from the street, then stood there with her.

Minh's whole body was covered by a white sheet except for his feet. Blood mixed with brain tissue splattered a few yards away from his head. Mai Lan stared at his feet. Those feet she had held them so often during his illness when he lay on the couch in their living room. She remembered every contour, the plumpness of the soles, and the large width, which called for wide shoe sizes. They were now still. As still as her life would be from now on.

She stood there she didn't know how long. The sun was near its zenith now. The officer had left. The sun poured over her shoulders, but she did not feel its heat. She did not feel any change coming from the outside world as if eternity had caught up with her. In an instant, she had been transported to another world, and she was the only one there.

"My darling, where are you now?"

No answer came, just her and a blank wall. All of a sudden, a thought planted itself in her consciousness. *Where are my kids? Oh no, I have to tell them. How can I tell them? What to do? Someone tells me what to do.*

She looked around. She was the only one standing in the parking lot. The officer was gone. Now shaking with apprehension, she walked back to the office.

Mai Lan, don't think too much. Go retrieve your kids. Whatever happens, you still have them. She drove to their school, sat in with the chaplain who waited patiently for her to be ready, then walked with her to the classrooms to pull Mike and Malia out.

That evening, Mai Lan spread a sheet on the living room floor, and the three of them settled there for the night. She waited for Mike and Malia to fall asleep, then knelt down and prayed, "Oh, God, please help me raise my two children to be good persons of value to themselves and to other people."

The days followed each other in a blur. Mai Lan tried to remember events leading up to Minh's suicide. Where did she err, and to what extent drove him to such an unthinkable act?

After the visits to Dr. Stein, Minh proposed for the family to move back to New Zealand. She recalled exactly that moment. She was at the kitchen sink doing the dishes. He was standing next to her. The words came very succinctly, without any explanation or elaboration.

"Do you want to move to New Zealand?"

She was too far gone, too spent to answer. The letter from her lawyer was delivered to Minh's office. She could not remember how many times she had gone over that letter.

Hawaii is a no-fault divorce state. The justification for divorce is that the marriage is irretrievably broken, which means that one party asserts there are irreconcilable differences. To Mai Lan's relief, the custody of the children was complemented by adequate visitation rights of the noncustodial parent, and joint custody might be considered. She had always wondered if Minh's position in the community and his good works would ensure he received custody. She was just a housewife with an ordinary job in nursing. The lawyer had assured her custody was usually awarded to mothers unless their lifestyle or circumstances were deemed unfit for child-rearing.

After receiving the letter, Minh did not engage in any discussion. He added more travel to his schedule. He was in much demand as a speaker for many refugee resettlements. From time to time, postcards arrived with his declarations of love for her and the kids, which left her cold. She had been functioning like a zombie for as long as she could remember. This zombie state had eased off recently after her decision to ask for a divorce. She was not about to fall into it again.

Several months passed by. One day, Minh told Mai Lan his office had been broken into, though nothing was missing. This happened a few more times. He was sure someone was trying to intimidate him in some way but couldn't think of any reason why.

Mai Lan couldn't help but remember the episode of the letter from the cousin in North Vietnam. In spite of reassurance from the private eye company they hired to investigate, the dark karma cloud had not vanished from their lives. Was someone trying to pressure Minh into revealing a dark secret about his relationship with the sister-in-law of the high-ranking leader of the Vietcong?

Now it was not only Mai Lan teetering on the edge of the abyss. It seemed like Minh joined her in the chaotic world of uncertainty, fear, and hopelessness. All of a sudden, Minh's mind stopped functioning. Forced to resign from his position in the company and to refuse all speaking engagements, Minh started seeing the psychiatrist instead of Mai Lan. She was the one driving him there. It was a 180-degree turn from last year.

Word of his despondency got around. Inquiries and good wishes poured in from friends, even from strangers, then slowly dwindled as time passed by.

Minh spent his days lying on the couch and staring at the ceiling while his wife and kids went about their daily lives. Divorce was now out of the question. Dr. Stein became their only support.

Then Minh seemed to have enough of his vegetative existence and stopped eating. Mai Lan used her lunch hour to come home and put a few tablespoons of food into his mouth. He refused to continue after those first spoonsful. He also stopped speaking.

So when Mai Lan got news that his two cousins would be visiting from Canada, she was elated. Minh had spent part of his childhood with these cousins, and they knew each other well. Could their visit rekindle some memories and a sense of well-being? Could he spend some time at his parents' place so that he could have some companionship while she was at work and the kids in school? He did not leave any written last words. That fatal morning, he said to Mai Lan, "I wish you well with your beau. Please take care of Mike and Malia."

She just looked at him and left, wondering what he meant.

Now his parting words seemed to come to life. She didn't quite understand the part about the beau, but she certainly would take care of the kids. One of her very favorite movies was *Gone with the Wind* in which there was a scene where Scarlett O'Hara tried to make a living after the war at the plantation of her parents. She was seen digging in the dirt, then lifting her fist to the sky to swear that she would never be hungry again. Likewise, Mai Lan swore that as long as she lived, she would dig her hands into the ground and do whatever it took to feed herself and her kids.

CHAPTER 12

A New Life

*And we know that in all things God works for the good of those
who love him, who have been called according to his purpose.*
—Romans 8:28

The air was still. The sun's rays had settled on the treetops. The quiet peace of the hour seemed to rise from the land and seep into Mai Lan's consciousness even as she resolutely continued to dig the weeder into the ground. She had been in the backyard working on the weeds since the morning. Suddenly, the air parted for a voice to come through.

"It's getting late. Why not quit and get some rest?"

Startled, she looked around. No one was to be seen. She looked down at the grass and continued weeding.

Suddenly, she felt tickling on the tips of her fingers. Something was crawling around her right index finger. In a panic, she yanked the glove off. A bee flew out.

How can this be? I've had these gloves on for some time. There was no bee crawling around in there. What's happening?

Mai Lan looked around. The yard was perfectly still. The sun was still on top of the trees. No one to be seen. Heart beating fast, she gathered the gloves and the weeder and hurried inside.

I must be hearing voices again. But I'm sure I'm not going crazy. Who talked to me? God help me. Mai Lan, just listen to the voice, whatever it is. You have been working all day.

That she was able to dig weeds all day was by itself a miracle.

She never imagined she was capable of such a feat. She usually did not have such stamina. Where would she get the muscle strength to proceed from one side of the yard to the other? The transition from desk to yard work had been too sudden. However, Mai Lan was no longer surprised at all the unusual things that happened to her now.

*****

"Mrs. Nguyen, this is Bob. I am a friend of your husband. We met when he was on his mission to deliver a speech to the refugee community in San Jose. My wife and I are just visiting, and we would very much like to meet you for a chat."

"Of course, you can come by tomorrow."

So Bob and Marie visited the next day. They said nice things about Minh and how uplifting his talk was to the community in San Jose. Mai Lan was glad to have company. After all the commotion of the first few months following Minh's suicide, she was practically left alone. She just listened to the two friends without saying much. She was glad to, again, be with her husband by listening to these strangers talk about him. Slowly, old memories took her back to happier times when she and Minh took walks in the neighborhood or marveled at beautiful vistas on their vacation trips. She was so immersed in her inner world that she had no reaction when Marie suddenly got up and without any invitation headed straight for the bedrooms, giving herself a tour of the house. When Mai Lan realized how odd this stranger's behavior was, Bob and Marie headed for the front door and left after a few parting words.

Several days later, they called. "Mai Lan, this is Bob again. The water is flowing backward."

Mai Lan put the receiver down. Either she was crazy, or Bob was. *What was the purpose of their visit? Was the water flowing backward a code phrase for some secret dealing? Were they really Minh's friends?*

For lack of a logical explanation, she decided to file the incident in the back of her mind. Her life had turned upside down ever since Minh left. She had lost her job and worried frequently about the kids.

Mike did not go to school unless he was wrapped in his father's raincoat, and Malia's writing got so small that her teachers complained about eye strain when going over her homework. The whole family moved around in a trance, pursuing their activities out of habit. Absent from their days were light talk and laughter. Mai Lan concentrated on maintaining the household and tending to her children's needs.

They tried to help in their own way. Mike mobilized his friends to plant a hedge of mock orange bushes to shade the west side of the house. Malia dug up some sow bugs from the backyard and raised them in a shoebox as part of a class project on how to care for pets. Mai Lan was sure Malia's classmates wrote on dogs and cats, not sow bugs, but her daughter knew enough about mother's mental anguish not to burden her further with the care of a cat or a dog.

Mai Lan continued to fret.

When will we see the end of the tunnel? How much longer can we survive on our savings?

Then the Vietnamese community turned against her. When Minh was alive, she was greeted warmly when they attended community events. No invitations came now. What's more, acquaintances pretended not to see her when they spotted her shopping in Chinatown. Someone even crossed the street just to avoid her.

So what's new under the sun? Rumors are probably flying that he took his life because of me.

On the other hand, Mai Lan's neighbors pitched in to help her. Mike and Malia got rides to school with them. From time to time, Mai Lan found fruits and veggies on her doorstep in the morning. Mike spent most of his weekends at the homes of close friends. Malia was often invited to sleepovers by her classmates. For Mai Lan, solace came from filling up her days with activities. Her life also filled up with Corky's presence. It seemed like he went away for a long time, then suddenly reappeared when she was at the nadir of despair and loneliness.

Besides the yard, the kitchen was her favorite place to retreat to. She felt secure there, fixing meals for her family while trying to make sense of what was left of her life in the aftermath of Minh's departure.

One day, her routine took an unexpected turn with Corky acting as a coach.

A lizard peeked at her from under the microwave, half of its body showing. It was about two inches long, so young that its thin pale skin revealed a bunch of organs bulging underneath. The pale greenish hue on its back gave way to a light brown over the rest of its body. It was a common lizard. Its head was comparatively big for such a tiny body. Its black eyes were like two tiny buttons staring at Mai Lan.

"All I need is a lizard in here leaving me droppings to clean up. Can you think of all the droppings he will leave around the house when he grows up? After that, he will make babies, and I will have to deal with baby lizard messes? Corky, did you send me this lizard? I cannot handle lizards."

Corky sighed. "You can always kill it. Just crush it."

"I can't do that! What a horrible thought!"

"As an alternative, may I suggest that you catch it and release it in the yard?"

By now, the lizard was completely out from under the microwave, almost to the edge of the countertop. Mai Lan tore off a piece of paper towel, wrapped it loosely around the lizard, and gathered the edges together. The lizard ran out from under the paper, then stopped, staring at her. When she swooped the paper down, the lizard again ran to the edge of the countertop and made its way to the stove. She swooped down again, and the lizard escaped again.

"How stupid of me. The paper is too stiff."

She reached for a plastic bag and swooped down again. The lizard ran again, then stopped and stared at her. She looked back in utter defeat.

Corky pitched in, "Ignore the lizard. Go back to your cooking."

She peeled the onion, chopped it fine, then turned around to look for the lizard. He was still on the countertop, staring at her. She peeled a clove of garlic this time, then washed some lemongrass.

"By the time I finish, the lizard will have disappeared."

No disappearance took place.

"Corky, what do I do?"

No answer. Corky must be out shopping or something.

"I cannot kill it. Looks like it's a male lizard." Though she had no idea what male lizards looked like versus female ones, she decided it must be male.

"My God, what do lizards eat? Mosquitoes? Flies? Maybe cockroaches? I only see one or two roaches in here from time to time."

Corky's voice penetrated the quiet of her mind. "I'll feed the lizard. You can get a small cup and fill it with water for him to drink."

Mai Lan complied. "For the life of me, I don't know what will come next. Maybe I should find a name for the lizard?"

"May I suggest Lizard with a capital *L*?" Corky was helpful again. Mai Lan remained mystified by the presence of Corky. With as much certainty as she knew that the earth revolved around the sun or that laws of gravity governed this world or that she was a human being made of flesh and born of her father's spermatozoid meeting her mother's ovum, she knew that Corky did not emerge from her brain, however far off her thinking could be at times.

Who was Corky? He was only a voice. He was often helpful though in a most irritating way. He made comments constantly on her daily activities, which made her feel as if she had regressed into infancy although they turned out to be always to the point. He was present day and night although his voice was audible only at appropriate times. In this way, she learned to follow his lead and reacted to him as if he was a family member. When his directives proved to be too much, she turned away; and when frustrated over what seemed impossible to do, she either shut herself up or let out a string of obscenities.

He waited patiently for her to calm down and seemed to disappear for a while. But he always came back. Her life had changed after that night when she knelt down to ask the Lord to help her bring up her kids. A neighbor, Suzanne, who lived two blocks away, seemed to always be at her doorstep when she felt down and out of sorts. Suzanne was well-known in the community for her Christian faith and her good works. She brought comfort when Mai Lan needed it most, fresh ideas on what to do. Usually when Mai Lan felt like she couldn't go on anymore, Suzanne was at the other end of the phone or at her doorstep with helpful advice.

Then Suzanne talked about God, whom she worshipped, and Mai Lan had many questions about Jesus. One day, Suzanne brought a Bible, saying it had all the answers to Mai Lan's questions, including the solution to Mai Lan's woes.

Mai Lan needed to find ways of getting out of her impossible situation.

Her work history was good enough that she could find a job wherever she applied. She was hired, worked a few days, then was fired. Her mind was obviously not on her work.

After realizing that she was not going to be employed anytime soon, she started digging weeds. Hopefully the weeds in her life would disappear too.

The Bible that Suzanne brought became a friend. It gave her a new way of looking at life, a new faith in the future.

It also brought back memories of praying for toys as a child, which netted her and her siblings toys at Christmas. It brought back memories of Christmas songs at the main cathedral in Saigon and following her friends there for midnight service on Christmas Eve. There was beauty in the hymns, which she did not find in the monotonous mantra recitations at the Buddhist temples. There was beauty in the worldview described by the book—a way of life that seemed so selfless it could not possibly exist.

Mai Lan started attending Suzanne's church with a neighbor who was also single.

"My dear friend, who knows? We both need husbands, wouldn't you say so? There must be men in church who can make nice husbands—one for you, one for me."

With time, they discovered there were no husbands to be found. Instead, surprises came in small and big ways. No matter how high the burner was on, the soup never boiled over.

One day, Mai Lan pulled a fish out of the refrigerator. The fish had been in there for a few days—its flesh was grayish; its eyes sunken. A faint odor of the sea wafted through her nose like the whisper of the sea. It had very subtle notes of rotten fish mixed with the aroma of the vast expanse of salt water, which she remembered from her childhood days of vacationing by the sea in Vũng Tàu. Not the smell of clean water but an intimate smell that brought back good memories.

For God's sake, do away with your memories, would you please? You have a meal to get ready. This fish is no good. It's not that bad, though. You don't have a lot of money to spend now. Besides, it's too close to dinner time to run to the store.

She started cleaning the fish.

I can mask the odor with a lot of garlic.

She reached for the cloves.

"You have too much garlic there," Corky injected.

Some of the garlic cloves flew onto the floor.

"Corky, you again. You are not human. How do you know how to cook?"

Mai Lan reached for the jars of salt and pepper.

When she looked back at the fish, her eyes almost popped out. Its color had changed from grayish to ivory white, the beautiful translucent white of a fish just caught. The smell was now the smell of the sea here in Hawaii, the clean smell of the vast ocean with rolling blue waves and dancing points of light.

Miracles kept happening in her life. Nothing big, but it seemed like God was with her daily. In her loneliness, He was a constant and His presence kept her going while relatives and friends seemed to have disappeared.

Tears came trickling down her cheeks.

Corky, thank you. Who are you?

*****

It was a beautiful morning. Upon waking up, Mai Lan's ears kept hearing an order that repeated itself: "Mai Lan, send two thousand dollars to this refugee organization. Your husband left a remarkable legacy to the Vietnamese community of Hawaii, and it befits you to continue it."

Astonished that the Holy Spirit would ask her such a thing while she was in the dumps, she nevertheless wrote the check.

"I am not through yet with these strange occurrences. Lord, whatever happens, I will trust you."

CHAPTER 13

The Pardon

"The Lord's Prayer"
Our father in heaven
Hallowed be thy name
Thy will be done
On earth as it is in heaven
Give us this day our daily bread
Forgive us our trespasses
As we forgive those who trespass against us.

All of a sudden, a sharp pain pierced Mai Lan's thigh. She jumped up and tried to massage it away. It was like a knife's blade slanting into her flesh, but it quickly faded into a dull ache and stayed there in spite of her kneading her thigh vigorously. From her experience with sciatica during her last pregnancy, she knew that this pain definitely did not come from any nerve malfunctioning, as far as she could tell, or from her muscles. They remained soft.

"Damn it, it still doesn't go away."

"Mai Lan, go to your phone book and look up all the numbers for the nursing homes on the island. Your mother-in-law is in one of them."

Stupefied, Mai Lan reached for the phone book, hoping the pain would go away when she complied with the voice, no matter how strange the directive was.

As she pored through the nursing home numbers and copied them into her notebook, the pain disappeared.

"Hello, I am looking for a Mrs. Tam Nguyen, who was recently admitted to your facility."

"Hello, do you have an old lady by the name of Tam Nguyen, admitted there recently?"

"Hello, my mother-in-law's name is Tam Nguyen, and she was recently admitted to a nursing home. Is she there?"

"Yes, ma'am, we have a person by the name of Tam Nguyen here."

The answer came through clearly at the other end of the line when Mai Lan reached the eighth nursing home on the list.

"Could I come for a visit?"

"You certainly are welcome to come."

"I'll call you back in a couple days."

Still stunned, Mai Lan sat motionless for a while. How could such a thing happen? She had not seen her in-laws for years. They lived with their daughter after Minh's passing. Mai Lan visited a couple times at the beginning of her widowhood, then stopped. The visits were rather formal, both sides feeling uneasy because of the circumstances surrounding Minh's death. There was definitely no love lost between the survivors of his suicide. She heard about her father-in-law's demise through friends. By that time, she had lost contact with her in-laws for so long that she was neither invited to his funeral, nor did she want to attend.

Now she had this unusual pain and received a tip from the heavens to get back in touch. Things kept happening in her life for which she had no explanation.

Why in the world would her mother-in-law end up in a nursing home? She had been so close to her daughter. *Well, I will find out when I visit*, Mai Lan thought.

The nursing home was perched on the flank of a hill not too far from Chinatown. It was surrounded by a high wall. One could follow the wall around from the parking lot and find that the building had no opening to the outside except at the entrance. Visitors would have to stop there and announce themselves to a guard.

What a formidable fortress! I bet people in here feel like they are in a prison. Mai Lan announced her visit.

"Please enter."

The gate opened. Mai Lan's idea of a prison eased somewhat when she walked along the gardens separating the residents' living quarters. There were shades alternating with sunny areas. Tall coconut trees and flowering shower trees stood over bushes of hibiscus and rows of ferns. Mother-in-Law's unit was at the end of the garden.

"Mother, I come to see you."

Mother was at the door. She squinted her eyes, then opened them wide and burst into tears. Mai Lan stood still, stunned by the reaction.

Mother grabbed her arms while sobbing loudly. "Your sister put me in here. She does not want me to live with her anymore."

"Mother, please don't cry now." Mai Lan held her hand and led her to the couch. "Tell me what happened."

"They decided to buy a bigger house and ended up choosing one on the side of a mountain. What's more, the house could only be accessed by a steep walkway with twenty steps made of cut stone. No way could I negotiate those steps. So they put me in here."

The words came in staccato through her sobs. Then the sobs died down.

"Oh, thank you so much for coming to see me. I am not abandoned here by myself."

"Doesn't anyone come to check on you?"

"Your sister still comes."

"How often?"

"Two or three times a week."

Mai Lan breathed a sigh of relief. Mother always had a knack for drama. The situation was not so terrible. "What does she do when she comes?"

"Oh, she brings me veggies and cooks and does the dishes and some other cleaning."

"So she takes good care of you. It's not like she abandoned you."

Mother remained quiet, staring into space. She seemed to have forgotten the presence of her daughter-in-law. In the stillness of the apartment, time seemed to stop.

Mai Lan looked around, then looked at Mother. She had aged—her eyes were more sunken, and the light which used to be there had left.

Suddenly she seemed to come alive. "Mai Lan, I apologize."

"What for?"

"Oh, I do apologize."

"Mother, what did you do?"

"How do you know I am here?"

"Jesus told me to come. He gave me signs to look for you, so I called the nursing homes to find you. I haven't seen you for so long. How are you doing now?"

"Oh, I apologize."

"Mother, what's bothering you?"

"I never told you, but ever since I set foot in this land, I told your husband to divorce you."

Mai Lan was speechless. She knew mother did not like her. She had experienced enough of her cruelty when they lived together under the same roof even when they lived separately, but she could not, in a million years, fathom that Mother would ask Minh to divorce her. Didn't she think of the children, her children, Mother-in-Law's grandchildren? Why would anyone want these kids to have their parents separated?

"Why did you do such a thing?"

Mother looked at her fiercely. "You know that way back then when I was only sixteen years old, there were two suitors who asked my parents for permission to marry me, don't you? It turned out I liked one, but I was forced to marry the one I didn't like. This made my life miserable ever since. I absolutely do not want my children to fall into the same trap. Why should your husband be left to suffer the same condition? Anyone who is not happily married should have a divorce and be free to start over again."

Mai Lan stared at her with uncomprehending eyes. The words sank in after a while. Mother had to be crazy. Didn't she know that Minh and Mai Lan were in love with each other?

Apparently not.

"You only marry him because both families match in social standing and level of wealth. I know you don't love him. He shouldn't be trapped in such a marriage, do you hear? I also knew you were unfaithful to him."

"Mother, I didn't do such a thing. How can you say something like that?"

"Oh yes. You are too pretty to be content with a handicapped man."

"But he only had a limp when he walked. Besides, being handicapped is not a sin. He was handsome!"

It was Mother's turn to stare at Mai Lan with incredulous eyes.

"Well, when after all these years you didn't remarry, I figure out you probably didn't have anyone on the side."

"Mother, I must confess to you that, at times, I found being married to your son was so unbearable that I had thoughts of looking for someone else. There was a time I wanted to escape somewhere with the resident who was working at the clinic where I worked. I never got the courage to let him know I was in love with him, though, and nothing happened.

"But you know what, whether I really did have a boyfriend on the side didn't matter. Your son and I never trusted each other enough to be honest and recognize that we had some awfully troubling problems. Remember when we saw the psychiatrist? All that time, I talked about how I hated you, and he just sat there, saying nothing. Didn't say a word about you wanting him to leave me.

"I just know now that he feared so much living without me and his two kids that he chose to remain silent and bear all his suspicions of me. Now that I remember, he honestly thought I had a boyfriend. Do you know that the morning he said goodbye to the kids and me before he jumped from your lanai, he said for me and my boyfriend to take good care of the kids? I just didn't pay attention. I thought he was delirious because he had not eaten very much for so long."

Mai Lan and Mother sat side by side without moving for a long time, each lost in the recollections of their mutual loss.

"There's something else I want to say to you, Mai Lan. I thought you poisoned my son. There was no reason why he should have gone downhill the way he did. I told the police you poisoned him. They even asked me if there was someone in our apartment the day he died, somebody pushing him from the lanai. I said no and that he died because you poisoned him."

This time, Mai Lan refused to look at Mother. There indeed was nothing else left to experience on this earth. Mother's thoughts were so incredible that they bordered on the ridiculous. Mai Lan poisoning her husband? And yet mother's thoughts were not without consequences. Now Mai Lan knew why Bob and Marie materialized out of thin air and visited her. So they were cops on a mission to investigate if she had indeed poisoned her husband.

"Mother, do you know that right before Minh got so sick, he told me someone repeatedly broke into his office leaving the door unlocked and yet not taking anything? That was probably the cause of his illness. He was under tremendous pressure from an invisible enemy that he couldn't identify. That enemy pursued him relentlessly. He suspected the CIA was after him due to his work with the community, to investigate whether he had ties with the Vietcong. Nothing ever materialized from such fears. All I know is he got sick.

"I know, though, in my heart that he sacrificed himself jumping from your lanai so he wouldn't become a burden to me and his children. That morning before he jumped, he told me to take care of the kids. Mother, I don't want to bring up the past anymore. Minh has been gone for a long time. I have my life to live now. So do you.

"It seems like today is the day for confessions, so I apologize to you, too, because way back then, when your son and I were just engaged, I promised you we would go back to Vietnam after we got married, but we never did. I knew when I made that promise that I would not go back. Who would want to go back to that hell? If you really loved your son and me, you wouldn't want us to go back either."

There was no response from Mother.

"Mother, I would say that left to me, I would flee this place forever. I really don't want to see you. You brought so much pain to everyone in your family. Remember the night I caught you tearing my beautiful picture? And when I cooked a nice meal for you, but you told me there was nothing to eat? When I toiled at catering to everyone in the family while you and your daughter sat around doing nothing?

"On the other hand, I thank you, Mother, for taking care of my kids when they needed someone to watch them after school. My schedule at work was so rigid I couldn't take off early to pick them up, so their dad did that and brought them to you, and you doted on them. For that I am grateful to you. Your son was a very tender and loving dad to his kids. He was the one taking them places and making sure they had some fun. I was more the one disciplining them. He made sure they had their ice cream cone after the visits to the orthodontist, and I used to scold them for wasting money on sweets they really didn't need. I wish those times could come back and I could see him again.

"You know, the kids are all grown now. Mike is on the mainland studying to be in theater work, and Malia is in college here majoring in biology. She put herself through school on scholarships, I don't have to support her in any way. I am so glad they turned out good.

"Do you know that the night when Minh jumped from your lanai, I knelt down and asked for help from God? I am Christian now. I am the treasurer/secretary for the local Vietnamese church. Jesus teaches his followers this prayer called the Lord's prayer. I will say it now so you know it too."

Mother still sat motionless, looking straight ahead.

Mai Lan bowed her head.

Oh, Lord, in heaven
Hallowed be thy name
Thy kingdom come, on earth as it is in heaven
Give us this day our daily bread
Forgive us our trespasses
As we forgive those who trespass against us
Lead us not into temptation
But deliver us from evil

"Mother, I am not perfect. Your son brought my family to America, and I am forever grateful to him for saving them from the horrible burden of communism. I am not without fault. I do need the Lord to forgive me, so I will come and visit twice a week to help your daughter take care of you. I can do some cooking and do the dishes and some cleaning for you.

"Mother, as far as I can tell, your daughter didn't abandon you, and neither will I. I will come again."

EPILOGUE

Spring Eternal

So now faith, hope, and love abide, these three:
but the greatest of these is love.
—1 Corinthians 13:13

Guard your heart above all else, for it determines the course of your life
—Proverbs 4:23

South Vietnam has two seasons, hot and hotter. There is no spring to speak of. According to the calendar, however, spring comes around Tết, the Lunar New Year, about January to March. More flowers can be seen in the markets, the weather is somewhat cooler, and people seem to enjoy life a bit more.

And yet Vietnamese literature is full of praise and excitement about spring. From "spring just arrived in the green fields" to "fresh spring, beautiful spring, spring blooming in our souls, eternal spring," odes to the season filled up tons of books, and songs are heard daily on radio, TV, and in homes, blaring in the streets or piping out of sound systems in restaurants.

When growing up, Mai Lan often let her mind wander through those images of spring while dreaming of springs elsewhere, where real springtime occurred in the succession of the seasons. Now that she had practically been around the world, as the childhood gift from

Jesus had predicted, she knew the tremendous anticipation of waiting for spring and the elation that came when it arrived.

A very special spring warmed her heart recently and came from an unexpected source. When she described her as spring, the response always was "She is no spring."

To get to this source, one had to climb all the way up a mountain overlooking Pearl City.

The road began by the Pacific Ocean, then crossed busy shopping centers and crowded apartment buildings for working people. Slowly, it climbed suburbs with single-family dwellings that grew more and more expensive and beautiful as one neared the summit. Near the top was a field of grass dotted with tropical trees—coconut mingled with mango, lychee, kukui nut, breadfruit, and tamarind. Sprinkled among the fruit trees were poincianas, bougainvillea, plumerias, and shower trees. When they were in bloom, it seemed like spring was everywhere on this land.

At the very top were several old buildings that served as headquarters for some of Hawaii's developmentally disabled people. Mai Lan drove up there every day. In her spare time, which was not much, she liked standing on the mountain and letting her gaze sweep over the landscape onto the vast expanse of the Pacific. Water and sky blurred together at the horizon. Moments like these brought her very close to the Creator. Indeed, almost every one of her coworkers felt like they were the chosen ones up here. The work was tedious, requiring a lot of patience and compassion but satisfying and fulfilling to the soul in the end.

Perhaps Katie was also chosen by God. She had a pair of beautiful brown eyes shaded by long curly eyelashes. Every time she laughed, her eyes shone bright. Those eyes were the only beautiful things in her body. Her mouth was rather large and had thick lips. When she did not close them, saliva started running down her chin. Her spine curved due to scoliosis, making one side of her body higher than the other. Her left arm hung limply with contractures distorting her hand. She walked with a limp. Mai Lan was sure, though, that Katie was unaware of how she looked.

She had a sunny character. She almost always greeted Mai Lan with an infectious laugh. As soon as she saw Mai Lan, she would clap her hands and start uttering a series of guttural sounds without meaning. There were also times when she would get mad and slide at once onto the floor to throw a temper tantrum. When this happened, it took a long time to soothe her.

When Mai Lan first knew Katie, just watching her eat would bring pain to her heart. She always had a big towel placed around her neck first. Her food, although pureed, always oozed out of her mouth. Not much of it, but it happened constantly. In spite of the disgrace, she slowly ate until the very end.

Changes came with time. At first, she ended up in the hospital every two or three years for pneumonia. Then it accelerated to every year, then every six months. Then her doctor announced that her lungs were dotted with holes due to food morsels getting lodged inside them instead of going to her stomach. The decision was made to stop her eating and insert a tube into her stomach for nourishment.

They received her back at the center, this time to start a new life. They felt for her. She was only in her thirties. She looked more like a kid at times and certainly had no way to understand that she would never taste food in her mouth again. And the staff had no way to explain to her why such a calamity had descended upon her.

They poured the formula into her feeding bag before having other clients eat. Then they turned her back to the main part of the dining room and put her in front of the TV to watch her favorite cartoons.

One day they carried some fruit juice to put in her feeding tube to clear milk curdles that had started clogging the lumen. One of them announced that she would be given fruit juice. She jumped up, both hands to the sky, a big smile on her face. "No, we don't mean you will taste this juice. It will go into your tube."

Katie sat back and did not look at them. A hush descended. The utter nakedness and loneliness of the moment brought tears to Mai Lan's eyes.

That day, it must have registered in Katie's mind that her eating had to be the way it was. She did not eat like anyone else, and the food did not bring pleasure anymore.

Then time passed. With it, the horrible odor emanating from her body from all the decaying food in her lungs slowly dissipated. Her skin turned from a sickly, pale dullness to a light glowing pink. She moved faster. She looked prettier.

The staff no longer put her in front of the TV but had her join others in the dining room. When they prepared her feedings, her eyes lit up. She eagerly waited for them to hook up the feeding tube to her gastrostomy tube and open the clamp. She stared at each drop of formula dripping into the receiving chamber. Sometimes she would pull on one of the staff to sit by her. Other times, she would clap her hands and chuckle.

Mai Lan did not know whether Katie rejoiced at having her stomach fill up and the sensation of hunger go away or relished the presence of people by her side. She was certain, though, that Katie had forgotten the pleasure of tasting food.

Instead, Katie looked forward to her almost daily excursions: the beach, the shopping centers, or just sightseeing. At times when watching others get on the van while she had to stay back, she would slide onto the floor and throw a temper tantrum.

Katie did not have the splendor of the spring ladies in romance stories. Her appearance, aside from her eyes, had nothing spring about it. But when she smiled as she spotted Mai Lan approaching with the feeding apparatus, a whole springtime blossomed in Mai Lan's mind.

Katie's life, a life so bare in its utter simplicity and yet so full of grace in its acceptance of destiny, a life speaking of eternal spring—Katie's life, Mai Lan's life?

Today like any other day, Mai Lan prepared the feeding tube, carried it to Katie, hooked the formula onto Katie's tube, and opened the clamp. Katie pulled at Mai Lan's uniform. She sat down. Katie clutched Mai Lan's hand, and both of them sat looking at the formula dripping down. After a while, Katie put her head on Mai Lan's shoulder, and Mai Lan wrapped her arm around Katie's waist.

"Katie, peace be with you and with me too."

ENDORSEMENTS

Linda Liem has written a riveting account of her life in Vietnam and her move to Hawaii during the war. Though she immigrated to escape the horrors of the conflict, she found that she couldn't avoid them entirely, and new problems appeared to test her. This is a book about enormous mental and emotional challenges, about finding a new way after losing the old one. We exult with Linda Liem when she heals on her new spiritual path.

—Pat Matsueda, managing editor for MANOA, 1992–2022

Linda Liem's *From Vietnam to Hawaii: A Spiritual Journey* is an evocative memoir that reads like a novel. The challenges encountered by Mai Lan as a woman coming of age in the midst of the Vietnam War are faced honestly. The initial joys of her marriage to an educated man who returns to Vietnam from his job in Hawaii to seek her as a bride are touchingly recounted. Whisked off to a new life in Hawaii and an escape from the tragedies of war, she is confronted with new obstacles and dangers.

Despite traumatic developments in her new life in Hawaii that led to tragic outcomes, Mai Lan rises to the occasions to keep herself and her children on paths that, despite being fraught with difficulties, are promising for their future. Mai Lan's discoveries of the Christian faith lies at the heart of this tale of survival.

Among the pleasures of this book are the poetic and eloquent epigraphs that are placed at the start of each chapter.

—Joseph Stanton (professor emeritus at
University of Hawaii at Manoa)

Linda Liem's memoir is a prize. She has lived and now shares with us the story and details of a poignant and difficult journey. The details make the story real, the telling personal, and the experience unforgettable.

—Bruce Harless (founding pastor of Dong
Tam Baptist Church, Honolulu)

Linda Liem is a gifted writer with an attention-grabbing life story.

She paints a detailed picture of Vietnam during the war in 1968. In this memoir, she describes the terror, hardships, and sorrow of war. Her painful story also includes her romantic journey to Hawaii, which later turns sour. Amid all the suffering and uncertainty in Vietnam and Hawaii, Liem finds Christ, who teaches her to forgive those who trespass against her and provides her a peace that passes all understanding.

—Robert Miller (director of regional ministries at Hawaii Pacific Baptist Convention)

Linda Liem's novel opens with a young girl's prayer: "Oh, Jesus, please give me some toys!" Mai Lan is the protagonist, and it's through her eyes that we witness her life in Vietnam and in Hawaii.

Liem's description of plants and food—like the custard apple, a "taste of heaven"—grounds the story where it happens. This book tells a tale of how people survive jarring life changes—like war and suicide—and how they can thrive despite mental and physical illnesses.

—Angela Nishimoto (retired lecturer in botany and author of *Isabella's Daughter*)

ACKNOWLEDGMENTS

I cannot thank enough all the people who helped me in the writing of this book. Without them, this story would not come to life. They include Pat Matsueda, who helped with the first editing work, encouragements and suggestions for improvements; Angela Nishimoto, who picked out the details that needed corrections; Pastor Bruce Harless, Pastor Robert Miller, and Professor Joseph Stanton for their endorsements; the Baptist Dong Tam Church for their interest in seeing this account of my life; and my family, especially my brother Quốc, for their support.

ABOUT THE AUTHOR

Linda Liem is a retired registered nurse educated at the University of Hawaii. She immigrated from Vietnam during the Vietnam War and practiced nursing in various fields, providing care for the people of Hawaii. She participated in receiving refugees from Vietnam after the war ended in 1975.

This book relates her cultural experiences navigating the transition from an old millennial culture to a multiethnic vibrant environment, with tones of mental illness and the extraordinary encounters with the beyond, resulting in deep faith in God and Jesus Christ.

9 798889 526723